To the patrons of the Kewaskum Public Library, I believe you'll enjoy reading this book. It will likely give you cause to reflect back on your own lives.
God bless you always!

Gary Beyer

You Must Answer This

Sharing Some of Life's True Feel Good Stories
and Not So Feel Good Stories

by Gary Beyer

D1495206

YOU MUST ANSWER THIS
(SHARING SOME OF LIFE'S TRUE FEEL GOOD and NOT SO FEEL GOOD STORIES)

Published by:
Beyer's Hope Unlimited LLC
2399 Golden Avenue, Oshkosh, WI 54904

Copies of this book may be purchased by contacting the publisher at beyershope@new.rr.com or by visiting the website at www.youmustanswerthis.com
You're encouraged to like this on Facebook at www.facebook.com/youmustanswerthis

Cover design and back cover photography by:
Rick Ramirez, Look! That's My Kid Photography
www.lookthatsmykid.com

Production efforts facilitated by:
John Steshetz, Proforma Printxx
www.proforma.com/printxx

Layout and print-ready work completed by:
Loralee L. Olson-Arcand, Word Services Unlimited
www.wordservicesunlimited.com

Printed by:
Seaway Printing Company Inc.
1609 Western Avenue, Green Bay, WI 54303
www.seawayprinting.com

Manufactured in the United States of America

With Love and Gratitude

This book is written as a lasting tribute to Julie, Mom and Dad, Doug and Shirley, Chelsea and Miss Kaylea Grace. It's been a labor of love and gratitude. Their tremendous impact on my life continues to serve me well.

I believe that the stories in this book deserve to be told. They are all true and expressed from my heart. This output's a compilation of thoughts from my life.

These stories are consciously not intended to be either chronological or sequential. The tapestry format of scenarios chosen here best supports the interwoven ebb and flow in each of our lives.

All thanks be to GOD for this wonderful experience. It is close to being rewarding beyond my comprehension.

Most humbly and respectfully,

Gary Beyer

Dedication

October 1st, 2013

Dearest Julie Ann,

Happy 25th Anniversary my love!! Words cannot adequately express how I feel about you. You've made my world very special; especially since we both formally made this life-long commitment to one another. I am always extremely proud and highly honored to call you my wife. It is with the deepest gratitude that I humbly dedicate this God-driven, heartfelt book, which comes from the depths of my soul, to you...my one and only Julie Ann. Any one who has the opportunity to read this in the future will irrefutably know that although I also wish to honor my parents, my brother, my sister-in-law, little Chelsea and Miss Kaylea Grace by writing this book...IT IS YOU, my Julie Ann who I wish to feature in its dedication.

You were supposed to hear, and heed, the voice which calmly told you, "you must answer this" after reading my personals ad in the newspaper back in the summer of 1987. As we regularly say...there are no coincidences. God bless you always and may God continue to bless our wonderful marriage.

With the sincerest expression of my love and devotion,

Gary Lee

Forward

I can still vividly remember reading a very riveting personals ad in the <u>Oshkosh Northwestern</u> in late July of 1987. At the time, I was sitting alone on the sofa in the living room of my apartment in Oshkosh. My spirits were very low because I was in the process of a very emotional and painful divorce. As I scanned the classified ads of the Oshkosh Northwestern, I spotted this personals ad and as I did a calm, androgynous-sounding voice said "You must answer this." I proceeded to get pen and paper and began to write a heart-felt letter in response to this personals ad. I was extremely upfront about myself and my personal life and included a school picture. I mailed the letter the very next day, but really didn't expect a response. However, as I placed the letter in the mail slot, a deep felt sense of peace came over me. Needless to say, that personals ad was written by none other than Gary L. Beyer, a young bachelor who was looking for that "special someone" to fulfill his life's dream of having a wonderful life partner.

This is how my relationship with Gary started, and what a relationship it became! Flash forward to October 1, 2013…we celebrated our silver wedding anniversary and Gary had just finished the rough draft of a book of personal reflections on life aptly titled "You Must Answer This". He asked me to write a forward for his book while we were eating a romantic dinner at a local restaurant, PRIMO! I am very proud to be able to claim Gary as my husband. He is truly my "soul mate", my "knight in shining armor" and my "prince charming" all rolled into one. I fell in love with Gary's intelligence, personal integrity and child-like enthusiasm for life. As I was reading over Gary's thirty-six narratives that comprise this book, I was struck by a common theme. Namely, the so-called events of our lives are more than just random events; they are all part of a larger plan for our lives. Also, even though our lives may be a series of "ups" and "downs", we can be assured that "hope" will be the glue that binds this tapestry of our lives together. Gary's narratives will give to the reader this very real sense of "hope". We must not forget that there is a "divine plan" for each of our lives. Gary's narratives truly reflect this central concept. Please be enlightened and entertained by my wonderful husband's narratives.

Sincerely yours,
Julie A. Beyer

Testimonials

"You can be very proud of what you've accomplished with this impressive book." –*SHIRLEY BEYER, my wonderful sister-in-law*

"Gary and Julie Beyer—Two of the most wonderful, caring and selfless people I have ever met—I feel privileged to have the honor of calling them good friends" –*GARY LUDWIG, friend since college*

"Having gone through some health issues myself, I respect people that keep their faith and positive attitude through adversity. I hope that readers will draw inspiration from Gary's ability in this book to share the moments that have shaped his life and his journey." –*DENNIS KRAUSE, well-respected Wisconsin sports personality, talk-show host and recent friend*

"Gary Beyer has been a personal friend of mine for a long time. He is a unique individual who thinks, feels, and speaks from his heart. In his later years Gary has suffered from physical problems that most of us have not only never experienced, but have never even heard of. Yet through it all he has maintained an upbeat attitude and a firm belief in God. I am sure that anyone who reads his book will find at least some of his experiences not only interesting but quite heart-warming as well." –*BOB SNYDER, long-time co-worker and friend since 1994*

"As a long time friend, I could tell Gary's passion intensified as he wrote these narratives. They have a message so enjoy them!" –*PAUL STEGER, friend since junior high*

"Gary Beyer is one of the most passionate people that I've ever met who has had a profoundly positive effect on many people's lives, including mine. His character and integrity are above reproach. I highly recommend **YOU MUST ANSWER THIS!**" –*STEVE ROSE, Author & Executive Producer, Coincidence or Godincidence TV Show and friend since early 2005*

"This man's journey of faith shows how an ordinary life leads to extraordinary experiences. A compelling book." –*GARY MADSEN, friend since junior high*

"Gary's life has been a very interesting journey with ups, downs and a few sideways moments. I'm happy that he's captured the essence in his memoir and I think you'll find it's a trip worth taking as well!"
—GREG IOTT, long-time friend and later co-worker

"I have the privilege to be acquainted with Gary and Julie as both long term friends and patients. They are two of the most loyal and trustworthy people I have known. I'm glad to see Gary's positive approach to increasing awareness of his condition. Best wishes for much success with the book."
—DR. RANDY WILD, friend since junior high and our eye doctor

"Gary, you are proof that determination, fortitude and the power of the Lord can move emotional mountains leaving only a flowered meadow of blessings. You have accomplished what many cannot. I am proud of you!!"
—NICKI JANSMA, HHP, CCT, CCEDSA naturopath, owner of Remedies Holistic Wellness Center and treasured health advisor and friend since early 2008

"Gary has amazed me at some of the things he has accomplished. When he puts his mind to something, it gets done, and done fast!" —JOHN STESHETZ, our friendship began when we each owned the same type of business... beginning in 2003

"From the day I gave you my trip to New Orleans, the many B-52's during budgeting, getting us included in the bonus plan and all the other times and issues it was great to work alongside you at Morgan all those years ago. A good friendship was created through that experience. Good luck with your book."
—MIKE MORRISSEY, long-time co-worker and friend since 1985

"Becky and I loved living in Oshkosh and one of the main reasons was the friendship of Julie and Gary. So many great memories, the Cubs game in Chicago, the trip to Vegas, the casino in Green Bay, and many more." —STEVE VESTAL, long-time co-worker and friend since 1994

"There are events in our lives that make us who we are. Sharing these stories gives us insight into not only Gary's life defining events, but how love, hope and perseverance can change our lives no matter the circumstances. A definite inspirational read. I hope your publication goes well."
—RANDY BONDOW, friend since high school

"Most people are frustrated by not seeing the "script" of their life. We don't see the meaning of the moments and this leads to loneliness and a lack of purpose. However, if you were given the answers for the test, you never would have studied or learned from your mistakes." –DR. ERIC GOWING, my rheumatologist and steady supporter

"Gary's narratives are very interesting and touching. I believe that God is in control and has a plan for each of us. We may never understand the reason why things happen as they do; but I trust that God knows the reason and he makes all things work out for our good." –DORIS PEITZ, long-time co-worker and friend since 1985 (She is now the Business Manager at the Paine Art Center and Gardens)

"I have known Gary both as a friend and a business associate, and his honesty and integrity are nothing short of admirable. I am proud to call Gary my friend. When Gary tackles a project he does it with great passion, the kind of guy who you'd want on your team." –ROBERT (BOB) JOHN, friend and owner of B. J. Clancy's restaurant

"I met Gary in 1971 at the University of Wisconsin – Oshkosh. We were both freshmen business majors – Gary in Accounting and I in Marketing. We shared many classes together and Gary was always very positive, enthusiastic and upbeat. Gary is that same person today, even after having endured serious illnesses, and the death of his father, mother and brother; all of with whom he was very close. I am very fortunate to have a sincere and honest friend such as Gary. The world would be a much better place if there were more "Gary's" in it." –GENE LANGENECKER, friend since college

"Julie, I just want to let you know I really enjoyed reading the excerpts from Gary's book! It is unbelievable how the timelines of some of the events seem to "coincide" with each other. I find those things happening in my life and am always reminded that there is Someone in Charge. I think of those things as "little pats on the back from God" for being in the right place at the right time"! Tell him Good Luck with his new adventure. I can't wait to see it in print!" –PAULINE HARPER, long-time co-worker and friend of Julie's

"Life meetings...we all travel unique roads in our lives...some we share with others some we have not shared yet...we met Gary and Julie Ann for a reason... the way we all live our lives is given to us by a greater being..we need to engage life...not just live it...discovering the purpose is the best part. Discover some of your own reasons for being ...Gary could be the Mitch Albom of Wisconsin... enjoy Gary's book and live...love, laugh, cry and share the ride with others."
–JIM "SUDZ" SZUDZIK, member of the Wisconsin IBM team since first being diagnosed with it in 2004. Sudz has become a good friend since we met in April of 2013.

"I have had the privilege of knowing Gary for only a few years but found those years very rewarding. When he asked me to read some of his life's stories that he was planning to have in the book I wasn't sure what to expect. Once I started reading I found I couldn't stop. It is so true that there is a plan and a purpose for life if you follow your beliefs and heart. Best Wishes."
–CAL WATTERS, friend and owner of Watters Plumbing

"Gary, I am truly amazed at your accomplishment in writing this book in such a short time. What an incredible memory you have to remember all these interesting and challenging life events and for being willing to share them with others. You and Julie are special and we are privileged to claim you as our friends." –DONNA WERCH, our friendship with Donna and her husband Dwain began when they became business partners of ours in 2003

"**You Must Answer This** gives you a glimpse into Gary's faith with life-stories that have given him much joy, and some that have given him great pain. I'm honored to be included in one of the stories that has brought him happiness. But I'm more honored to have him as a friend." –RICK RAMIREZ, friend and former co-worker beginning in 1994

"Gary, I really did enjoy reading this. I thought I knew you pretty well but learn so much more. You are an incredible person who like me always tried to look for the good in people and to stay positive. We are God centered and know he has so much to do with our lives unfolding." –LINDA DITTBURNER, long-time co-worker of Julie's and friend

Other Testimonials

"Gary Beyer has been a trusted friend of mine for over 40 years. When he informed me that he was writing a book about many of the events that have been a part of his life, both good and bad, and how those events influenced the path that he sets for himself today, I knew Gary would not only complete this task, but allow those events to educate and inspire others. He has always been this way. It's simply a part of his genetic makeup.

"Gary has always had this inbred determination, combined with an almost child-like enthusiasm for whatever life would throw at him. Always able to find the "sunny side" of life's foibles, he would not only learn from life's lessons, he would embrace the experience and share that with others. You will find exactly that in this book. That's what Gary is. It's simply his nature.

"I, for one, have never known anyone who enjoys the journey of life more than Gary. He treasures the good times, takes count of the blessings derived from them, and thirsts for more. And the bad times? Gary has a knack of taking on those struggles we all face, and somehow comes out the other side a better man. Not all can do that. Then he goes the extra step and shares it with others. Typical Gary.

"Gary has more obstacles in front of him, but I never worry about Gary. He identifies the obstacle, utilizes the assets and resources (including family and friends) to tackle it, and somehow keeps a smile on his face and unbridled confidence in coming out on top.

"I am honored to be able to call Gary a friend, and know this publication will touch and inspire you. That's Gary's way. All I can say is: Charge on, Mr. B!"
–GARY WEST, friend since junior high

"As Plant manager at Morgan door company I had to work with many different people and department heads on a daily basis. My least favorite department was always accounting (bean counters) because it seemed like their sole purpose in life was to report or find something that manufacturing was doing wrong in the plant. When Gary came on board at Morgan's my whole attitude changed, he was a manufacturing ally who was not only there to help us with our cost control in the plant but he was all about being a team player. He had a blue collar attitude that was so user friendly I never hesitated to call and ask him about almost anything plant or cost related. He was helpful and very professional at all times, and yet he had an uncanny knack of making work always fun. When Gary called me in his office and told me he was leaving the company I knew he would be irreplaceable, and you know what I was right!" *—MIKE FLANIGAN, long-time former co-worker and friend since 1985*

"Everyone wishes for a charmed life. The reality is life is not so easy. Along with the good, we have to deal with a variety of challenges. Illness, death of loved ones, loss of a job, unforeseen accidents, and conflicts with others provide us with an obstacle course that can seem insurmountable. How does one navigate through this and find happiness? Gary Beyer has faced these problems and through his attitude and perseverance he has found a way to take the bad with the good. He has created a model of how to live a life and absorb whatever comes our way. He has shown there is a way forward through hope, faith, and effort. He reminds us that the quality of our life is in the journey forward and how we face each experience gives our life meaning and value." *—DR. GARY DUBESTER, our dentist and friend for over 25 years*

Table of Contents

Always Remember The Words Of My Friend Steve Rose…
"THERE ARE NO COINCIDENCES, ONLY GODINCIDENCES"

ભ 1 ଓ
I'm SORRY TO HAVE TO TELL YOU This, But...

...we're bringing your son Gary to Theda Clark Hospital in critical condition. This is the very disturbing message that my mother was given when she answered a telephone call at close to 2:30 in the morning of Friday, March 23, 1979.

I'd been involved in a serious car accident that took place late the night before about a mile or so from my apartment in Berlin, Wisconsin. They were urgently transferring me to this larger, more suitably equipped hospital in Neenah where she lived.

I was working at Medalist Sand-Knit, which was located in the small, rural city of Berlin. It had a population of around 5,000 people back then. The Sand-Knit plant was located at the base of a hill which was close to the Western-most entrance to the city. The nearest larger city is Oshkosh, and it's about 25 miles to the east.

Sand-Knit was one of the many diverse divisions which made up Medalist Industries. It wasn't that well known outside of Berlin and the surrounding cities of Ripon, Green Lake and Omro. It is bordered by some unincorporated communities like Auroraville, Rush Lake and Waukau. What was incredible though was Sand-Knit, at that time, was the manufacturer of uniforms for most of the National Football League (aka NFL) teams. It also was the licensed producer of

Gary sporting the uniform of his favorite baseball team, the Milwaukee Brewers.

attire for about two-thirds of the National Basketball Association (aka NBA) teams. The majority of major college sports programs featured uniforms that were designed and manufactured by Sand-Knit. When I was there, three Major League Baseball teams proudly wore uniforms made by our company as well. They were the Milwaukee Brewers, the Chicago White Sox and the Houston Astros. If you ever had or have the opportunity to check out the Astros multi-colored Sunburst style jerseys, you'll never forget them. They were 'Cool' with a capital C and quite distinctive for their time.

Being an avid fan of professional baseball, football and basketball, this was a dream job for me. I also loved college football and basketball. Walking through the plant was always a treat. There were numerous sewing machines, imprint equipment, tackle twill lettering stations, knitting equipment and an art department to name just some of the highlights. The shipping department was always intriguing because our clothing went all over the country. We were officially known as "the designer for the pros." Orders came in from numerous sporting goods stores to satisfy the uniform needs of amateur and semi-pro teams throughout their respective coverage areas. Compatible casual clothing was produced here too. These types of sports related demands were being consistently met by this relatively small plant, which was quaintly located in a little town that is near East Central Wisconsin.

I was hired to be the Assistant Controller at this facility. I was close to earning my MBA and was taking associated classes at night. Working there was enjoyable. The people were very friendly and the environment was comfortable and family-like. I interviewed for the position in October of 1978 and was excited to accept the offer I was given. The salary of $10,000 per year was big money at the time. I was single and not involved in any type of relationship. I had my yellow Camaro and it was quite sharp. My time was my own and my wonderful mother was extremely proud of her youngest son. She represented my primary guy wire and supporter. I had been living with her in the home I grew up in. After my Dad passed away in 1971, it became good for both of us. I had moved away for a relatively short time in conjunction with my first job out of college, but had moved back after resigning from that position. Getting an apartment in Berlin was something I was looking forward to. I found a nice place; it was very nearby the Sand-Knit plant. The proximity was good but walking to work every day would have been a bit much. Driving to my office involved pulling out of the parking lot, getting to the main street, going straight for a short while and then heading down a pretty steep hill. My place was on the second floor, and it was very pleasant. There wasn't a lot for a single person to do there, but I commonly headed to either Oshkosh or back home on the weekends. When I went into Oshkosh for my evening graduate classes my normal intentions were to head right back after the class had finished.

One evening, a long-time friend of mine, Paul Steger, called me about getting together in Oshkosh. He said he was going there on Thursday night, March 22, 1979, because he wanted to pick up a few records at the Exclusive Company in town. We both liked music and I told him I'd meet him there. Work had been pretty busy and it sounded like a great idea. We'd later get some food and have a few drinks. I always enjoyed his company and figured this would be good for both of us. I left directly from work and headed east to Oshkosh. The weather was reasonable and I was looking forward to it. I met Paul at the record store and purchased the album *Breakfast in America* by the group Supertramp. I was already familiar with a few of their songs and was excited about getting it. We went to a place nearby and ordered a couple of their so-called 'Magnet dogs.' They were like hot dogs covered with tasty barbecue sauce which included some hamburger (I'm sorry if I've gotten you hungry). We then drove over to a bar nearby called Good Knights. I was drinking Lambrusco wine at that time. There was a friendly and attractive bartender working, named Diane, that I knew. After leaving Good Knights, we headed over to a very popular bar named Mabel Murphy's. It was like Christmas all year round there as the mirrors and less brightly lit atmosphere kept most people focused on one thing; which was having a good time. We visited some more and basically had an enjoyable evening. We said goodbye, and then I headed back to Berlin and Paul headed on to Neenah.

It was typical Wisconsin weather during this time of year. The conditions had worsened and the external environment had changed over to wet snow and then sleet-like precipitation as I was driving back to my apartment. We'd left Oshkosh about 11:00. Normally, Berlin was about 30 minutes from where I started from. On this particular night it was probably closer to 40 to 45. The first half of the trip back involved two-lane country roads that were pretty straight. As expected, I didn't run into much traffic the entire time. The second half of the ride became more bothersome. There were some curves along the way, but they were most prevalent the nearer I got back to town.

Less than a mile from reaching the city there was a particularly bad stretch and visibility had noticeably deteriorated. The terrain had periods of lowland accompanied by some variable dips and rises. I wasn't driving that fast and I detected a major set of vehicle lights coming from the opposite direction. The intensity of these lights seemed to appear out of nowhere as this vehicle was coming out of a low spot that was not yet determinable in my line of vision. It seemed to be a large truck of some kind and it was taking up considerable space on the road. I got scared and turned the steering wheel a bit towards the right; I then hit a chuckhole in the roadside and quickly turned the wheel back to the left. This is fortunately all that I remember about the accident. By the grace of God, everything else about it is gone. If it wasn't, I probably would have become averse to driving much again.

It turned out that it was a truck carrying 26 tons of sand that was approaching from the opposite direction. Upon contact, the front end of the car was dramatically compressed and the hood was driven back through the windshield. I was thrown to the passenger side of the car and was bleeding badly with considerable glass particles in my face and head. Luckily, I wore glasses. In this case if I had been wearing a seat belt, I may have been decapitated. This was definitely an exception though. I now always wear my seat belt and will encourage others to do so as well.

I'm told the driver called 911 for help and that an angel-like nurse from

Berlin Hospital worked incessantly to help get me stabilized. I never had the opportunity to thank either of them for their selfless help and consideration. I was taken by ambulance to the hospital, which thankfully was not that far away. They just didn't possess the necessary

My yellow Camaro after the accident.

medical equipment that I badly required at the time. Arrangements were made to have me transferred to the larger hospital that was located in Oshkosh. A CT scan and other specific services needed to be urgently performed on me. Back then, Theda Clark Hospital in Neenah was considered 'the cream of the crop' as far as ranked hospitals in our area. They were recognized for having the most state of the art medical equipment available.

I still feel bad about the trauma I put my mother, my brother and sister-in-law and my friends through, especially my mother who got the unnerving call. She certainly didn't deserve to experience that. When they called Paul to tell him what had happened and ask him about our evening together, he got pretty shook up too. He came over to see me when I was in Intensive Care. I suffered a punctured lung, a broken left clavicle, some broken ribs and a concussion with severe headaches for close to a couple of weeks. To this day, the pain associated with these headaches has been the worst pain I've ever experienced. They gave me absolutely no painkiller for a few days. When I got placed in a room, the metal sides were kept up on my bed. I also had a roommate. I can still remember consciously gritting my teeth while trying to squeeze one of these bars as hard as I possibly could so as not to disturb him during the night. Numerous contusions, bruises and banged up areas, that were attributable to being thrown around in the car, provided me with steady reminders of what had happened. Also, for quite some time small pieces of glass would come to the surface of my forehead as well as to other parts of my face.

It was thanks to my mother's efforts and her own creativity that these unbelievably painful headaches finally not only dissipated, but they disappeared. I was released to her care in a reasonably short time. I had a bunch of healing to do and she was a wonderful nurse. She's the one who came up with the idea of keeping a cloth tied around my forehead after I got home. All of a sudden, the headaches were gone. I was very thankful for this. In the hospital, she was asked to sign a release before an anticipated procedure could be done to deal with a collapsed lung. Thankfully, prior to beginning this procedure the lung issue resolved itself.

I was able to return to work on a part-time basis in about six weeks. I've definitely been truly blessed. A highly spiritual co-worker said to me shortly after I'd returned, "Gary, you've been kept alive for a reason." My family drove over to Berlin to take pictures of my treasured yellow Camaro. They went just a couple of days after the accident. It had been towed to a spot behind the West Side Garage in Berlin. When people saw these pictures they could not believe that anyone could have survived the associated crash, let alone not suffer any paralysis-type issues. The grace of God and my guardian angel are the reasons I triumphantly survived this accident. With the utmost humility, I'm (EXTREMELY THANKFUL) TO BE ABLE TO TELL YOU this story. Just one more thing, my brother searched to find me another yellow Camaro around the entire Fox River Valley. He found one at a car dealership in Kaukauna, about 40 miles north of my home town. They surprised me with it soon thereafter.

○ℛ 2 ℬ○
She's CLEARLY THE ONE FOR US, Miss Kaylea Grace

It became very clear on that cold and sunny Sunday afternoon which Julie and I spent in Antigo, Wisconsin. On this first day of February of 2009, we had been introduced to the future newest addition to our small family. There was absolutely no doubt or hesitation involved with our decision.

This attractive little cream-colored female with the white chest and paws had already stolen our hearts with her attentive and charming behavior and she wasn't about to let go of them either.

Julie and I met a little bit later in our lives and neither of us had any children from previous relationships. We both grew up with dogs and loved animals.

When I was a child we had a toy fox terrier named Tippy for a number of years. After her death, my Dad brought home a dog from a co-worker whose name was Shaggy. You can probably picture what she looked like and we just could not get her properly house trained. She was a discipline problem and her stay with us was not very long; she was given away. My mother raised a few litters of miniature poodles and I was able to see first hand how intelligent and loving they were. Fifi, the mother of these litters was quite the lady. She had the nicest personality and I couldn't imagine any dog being better behaved than she was. Her puppies were never around very long. Once the time came where they were ready to be on their own, they were snapped

Kaylea Grace as a puppy.

7

up pretty fast by either family or other prospective owners. My brother and sister-in-law selected the first male and named him Andre. Talk about a good dog! Her second litter had one puppy. My Dad and I fell hard for little Shelly. Of all of her puppies, she was the most feisty and sure was full of energy. Julie's first dog was medium-sized. It was an English springer spaniel she named Penny (aka Penny the Pooh). Her parents got her when Julie was nine years old and she lived another seven with them. She was liver colored on white and had penny-shaped spots on her back. After this, they got a black lab mix pup from a litter from her uncle's dog and named her Josie. When she was in her first marriage she became very attached to a short-haired black and tan dachshund named Betsy. Julie has some bothersome allergies and pet hair is one of them. This was important for us to consider in our selection of the type of dog that we believed would be best for us.

She never experienced being around poodles, but was open to the idea of owning one when we first talked about possibly getting a dog. She, more than me, was watching the newspaper and other advertising vehicles for "puppies for sale." In the summer of 1992 we had become pretty serious about bringing a dog into our home. My birthday falls on the first day of summer and we would commonly host a large party each year on one of the Saturdays nearest this date. The Thursday evening before one of these planned parties at our home, Julie had read an ad for toy poodles in the town of Markesan. This was located about an hour Southwest of us. We made an appointment to go see the dogs on Friday afternoon. When we arrived, there were a number of them to choose from. However, we were both quickly sold on this cute little silvery-black female who was the runt of one of the litters. We had brought the checkbook and a blanket. The decision was easy…we excitedly brought her back to her new home.

She was actually six months old at the time. She had been given the name of Susie but we changed it right away to Chelsea. The day of the party, the weather was extremely atypical. Our intention was to basically hold the party outdoors in our backyard. We had two guys hired to sing and play guitar. The setting was perfect, but the weather was not. It was so cold for late June. Thankfully, two friends who lived nearby went home and brought over their portable outdoor fire pit; it literally saved the day. But picture this, here's little Chelsea scared to death in her new environment. Julie became her steady caretaker all day.

Chelsea had a dream personality and we thoroughly enjoyed having her around for 16 wonderful years. People would ask us, "when something happens to Chelsea will you get another dog?" Our answer was consistently yes, but we were so attached to her that we knew losing her would be extremely difficult for us. She had to have most of her teeth pulled over the years and had become blind in both eyes. Regardless, she some how gummed her little bones and was actually able to get around pretty well for quite some time (despite coping with a sunken living room) in our house.

It had reached a point where we were facing a very difficult decision. Chelsea had been diagnosed with cancer and there was no turning back. Both my mother (when she was alive) and Julie's parents loved watching her. She'd been pretty easy to take care of if we went on vacation or went somewhere for a long weekend. This was no longer the case. During Julie's Easter vacation in March of 2008, we took my sister-in-law Shirley along with us to baseball Spring Training in Arizona. Julie's parents watched Chelsea and I was scheduled to see the Neuro-Muscular Specialist, for the first time, at the University of Wisconsin Medical Center in Madison. This was to be on the Monday after we returned. It was he who had communicated with me, via a mid-Friday afternoon telephone call on January 18th. He'd told me at that time that I'd been diagnosed with a very rare type of incurable muscle disease called Inclusion Body Myositis. This was confirmed only after the results from a laboratory analysis of my thigh muscle biopsy had been thoroughly examined.

The Saturday night before we were to be returning home Julie called to check in with her Mother. Her Mom quickly said, "Are you sitting down?" The look on Julie's face said that something was clearly wrong. She told her that Chelsea had passed away and that they'd taken her body to their vet. We hoped to be able to pick up her body early Monday morning and bring her to our vet's office to be cremated prior to leaving for Madison. We never got to say goodbye to her, but we believe this is the way it was supposed to be. We felt bad for Julie's parents because we knew this had to be very difficult for them too because they also loved little Chelsea. This was an extremely stressful period for us.

Once this happened we knew that it would be awhile before we'd be ready for another dog. She was like our kid. We loved her dearly and always tried to treat her with honor and respect. We always believed that God would help us to know when the time was right to seriously consider getting another dog. Then on Friday evening, January 30, 2009 (over 10 months later), Julie happens to read an ad for toy poodles in Friday night's <u>Buyers Guide</u> paper, but doesn't tell me about it. As I'd said earlier, I was raised with toy poodles and was pretty sold on them as wonderful pets. Our little Chelsea had gotten Julie hooked on poodles, too.

The very next day, we decide to visit our sister-in-law Shirley who lives in my home town of Neenah. While there, she incidentally asks if we'd thought any more about getting another dog. We hadn't discussed this for quite some time. Julie then tells of this ad she'd read the night before and you could tell that she was quite excited about it. She said there were two females and two males…and we were both sold on females. We had gotten Chelsea spayed and our intentions would be to do the same when we got another female.

We were both clearly ready to be serious about looking for another dog. I said let's go check them out tomorrow (which was Sunday, February 1st) and when we got back home I quickly called to be sure that it would work out. The breeder said this would be fine and we gave her an approximate time of arrival. She said she'd be looking for us. I then proceeded to make a list of potential female dog names on a small tablet. I asked Julie for any additional ones we should consider and we took the time to select one of these names. The choice of Kaylea was unanimous among a total of about twenty names. We decided a middle name of Grace would be an appropriate homage for my mother.

In the morning, we stopped at both Walmart and Petco and picked up some doggy items before heading the 100 or so miles north to Antigo. We knew that we'd be pushovers at this point. It was pretty obvious that we were both very excited about getting there. When we arrived we were greeted by the breeder and some barking little dogs. We came in, sat down and learned more about our possible options. The obvious choice was one special little girl. She just stood out. While we were there another couple came to the door to check out the available poodles for themselves. During this time,

Julie closely held onto (and wasn't about to let go) the one dog that had captured our attention. Fortunately, they didn't commit to buying her before we did; because it could've gotten a bit dicey then. The lady seemed to be leaning towards getting a male when she'd first arrived.

As when we drove to Markesan in 1992, we had our checkbook and a comfortable blanket along with us. Julie had already wrapped her up in the blanket and I wrote out the check to seal the deal. She was seven months old and they had named her Jenny. Home we went with our new little priceless blessing. She only weighed about four pounds and weighs just over five pounds now.

She's become quite the stress reliever too…half the time we're laughing at her cute traits; she views Julie as her playmate and commonly "barks her up" and innocently nips at her toes. Her regular spins and twirls are always evident when she gets excited about something. Talk about fast! Like Chelsea before her, she runs her regular circuits around the inside of our house. Unlike Chelsea, Kaylea is pretty much of an indoor dog. We live near

a wood line and there are owls, hawks, raccoons, etc. that show up frequently. We trusted Chelsea outside and kept a close eye on her but she was trained more than Kaylea has been in this regard.

Kaylea has truly become a caregiver for us as well. When Julie was suffering from a major back issue shortly before Thanksgiving of 2011, and then throughout the Holidays, she was right by her side. With the progression of my eye and muscle related issues she rarely lets me out of her sight. She's become Daddy's little girl alright. She consistently makes direct eye contact in a manner that we've never seen before and is always extremely

Gary with Kaylea Grace.

interactive. At least once a night she jumps up on the hydraulic lift chair that I regularly sleep in and proceeds to inundate me with kisses. She still sleeps on the heart-shaped pillow we'd bought before leaving Oshkosh that memorable day of February 1, 2009. Little did we know that we would be introduced to the precocious Miss Kaylea Grace. We've come to believe that she's an angel dog. There's one thing for sure though. She's CLEARLY THE ONE FOR US.

ಝ 3 ಖ
THE PEACE THAT PASSETH ALL UNDERSTANDING....WOW!!!!

I now understand what this truly means. It took me nearly to the age of 52 to actually experience it. That's right, it took me this long to finally experience it for myself. It is not associated with a mindset, nor is there a recipe to follow in order to realize it. I will tell you this though; you will understand what I'm talking about when you're blessed with its presence.

My wonderful mother Grace always put helping others before herself. She was unwaveringly devoted to her husband Clary and her two boys...a true matriarch. She also became fiercely independent over the years. Watching her decline from the onset of dementia/Alzheimer's was the most difficult thing I've ever been faced with. It brought on the most helpless of feelings and it became a real challenge for me to keep upbeat.

Mom was always the glue for our family. What I mean by this is that she was the one that enabled us to keep moving forward. I believe we all took her for granted, but this was probably because she represented our base and "most constant" anchor. She was always so strong and reinforcing. Like my Dad, she was redoubtable in character and upfront with the expression of her views on things.

She was the second oldest of six children. The oldest had moved to Michigan after she got married and Mom was to become the primary caregiver for both her mother and father. My father and her got married in January of 1929. It was the heart of the Great Depression and times were tough. Mom was to be just turning 17 in February. Dad was only 22. He worked in the foundry and Mom got a job at Carver's ice cream store.

When I was growing up, we'd head to Grandma's house in Oshkosh for a lunch-time meal nearly every Sunday. She was an awesome cook and would commonly serve these very tasty roasts with oven-browned potatoes and carrots (I'm sorry if I've made you hungry). My Dad was her favorite

Gary with his mother.

son-in-law and she'd be sure to have his favorite dessert of apple cream cake available, more often than not. She would usually make two pies from scratch and boy were they good.

I was raised in the Episcopalian faith. We attended church regularly, and I was an acolyte. I believed in God, but in all honesty had not developed enough of a relationship with Him. Dad was having his health issues and Mom had a hysterectomy. I consistently prayed to God, but in hindsight it was as more of an outsider appealing for help. I never questioned God's power, but hadn't adequately internalized my own relationship with Him.

Mom was always there to help my Dad during many of his heart condition flare ups and colon cancer complications; that were further burdened by a humbling colostomy and the tear-generating, painful cramps in his abdomen. My Dad passed away when she was fifty nine and I'd just finished my last year of high school. It wasn't a surprise, because we knew it was coming. Regardless of this, it did not make it any easier.

She stayed in the beautiful stone house that my father and brother Doug had built. It took them five plus years to complete; with both of them working stressful, full-time jobs. The home was unique for its time and a story was done on it in the Friday, July 1, 1960, issue of the local <u>Appleton Post-Crescent</u> newspaper. Cutting her large lawn and hand shoveling snow were always part of her routine. Doug and Shirley lived next door, but you could usually not get up early enough to get to it before Mom did. She recognized that they had their own stuff to deal with and didn't want to be a burden to anyone.

I always fought hard to help Mom keep as much of her independence as possible; typically erring on this side of most of the associated decisions. After recovering from two broken hips and detecting the onset of dementia; it had become very clear that she needed to be living in a less threatening environment. Mom had willingly, but reluctantly, agreed to stop driving her car. This was especially tough because this had been her primary means for getting out to talk with other people; while putting herself in some different surroundings for awhile.

Her house needed a lot of work to be done in it before it could be put up for sale. I don't know what we'd have done without the tremendous help from a former co-worker of mine. He is a very talented, part-time handyman whose name is George Woldt. His considerable skills and efforts enabled us to get this house on the market. The work began as Mom was recovering from her first hip replacement surgery. She stayed with Doug and Shirley for about eight weeks. Shirley especially helped her with her daily needs and it provided her with some great company during this time. We put up "welcome home" signs and treated her homecoming as a celebration. As much as she appreciated their care, she was glad to be back in her own home.

We'd been telling Mom that we were getting her home in a position to be listed for sale. She needed a second hip replacement, this time on her left side, right after Easter of 1997. This was only about six months after her first surgery. She ended up being placed in a rehab facility on the east side of Oshkosh for a period of time before being able to come back to her home. Her safety needed to come first and we'd been stressing this to her. After living in this home for over 40 years Mom was, understandably, not at all keen on leaving it.

Julie and I had been searching the Oshkosh area for the most appropriate place for Mom to move into. We moved her from her home to a nice two-bedroom apartment; which was only about five minutes from our home. The second bedroom was consciously used to display some of her various treasures and contained a desk and a couple of chairs to subtlely allow her to feel less cramped. She had a very nice, decorative shoe collection that we consciously featured in this extra room. I don't regret this move, but her condition was quickly reaching a point where she was requiring more daily assistance. It had become important for her to have more consistent contact with other people in her environment.

Thankfully, I had initially looked into a wide array of re-location options for our mother. We each recognized the fluidity of dementia/Alzheimer's and believed that there could be a series of moves involved before we found the right place for our Mom. We also were aware that moving was difficult for anybody; regardless of their age or circumstances. Our intention was to keep her subsequent moves to an absolute minimum.

Well, it didn't work out that way. There was a visually attractive, relatively new at the time, assisted living facility about one block from the apartment which Mom was in. It seemed to have everything. We underestimated one major thing though; Mom was the one who'd be living there and not one of us. She'd been put on a medication called Zyprexa during this time. I always tried to stay on top of things, but this was new stuff for all of us. Mom started falling in her room. I'd received two late night telephone calls that she was being taken via ambulance to hospital emergency. Something had definitely changed. She was also diagnosed as being dehydrated. Mom was always one who loved drinking water. I learned that this issue should definitely not be taken lightly. It's critical for this to be overcome. After the second fall, the facility would not allow Mom to return to it. An evaluator had come to Mom's apartment in September of 2000 to meet with her and I to determine her status and whether she was a candidate for admission to the assisted living facility. I was told that she passed their test. This was only December and we originally had to pay a $1,500 admission-type fee. They would not refund us this fee despite our formal request to do so. They gave us no consideration, whatsoever, for the extenuating circumstances.

Mom's only option at the time was to be transferred to another of their facilities. She was placed into a small, two-bed room with another person. The atmosphere here was much less appealing. Again, thankfully, I was prepared with a back up option. Mom was now formally recognized as having a greater level of dementia. I had previously identified, what appeared to be, a very nice dementia/Alzheimer's facility in walking distance from our home. I had already spoken with the director there and was highly impressed with her. It was time to re-visit this option. Another Alzheimer's facility was under the same operating umbrella as the assisted living facility that my mother had been living in for just over two months. We toured both of them as a family and we unanimously chose the former one. By the grace of God we were able to get Mom quickly re-located into, what became, a very pleasant and appropriate place for her to live.

She was able to spend the last four years of her life at this dementia/Alzheimer's facility. The directors and staff were wonderful to her. She became one of their favorites. One of the caregivers gave her the nickname of "Gracie Bean." I ended up fighting extremely hard to keep Mom there. Her funds were running out and the last thing you want to do is move an Alzheimer's patient when he or she has reached a certain stage in its advancement. Another major Godincidence occurred when we were able to keep her in this facility. I'm more proud of this effort than anything I'd ever previously accomplished in my life. I distinctly remember being told by an acquaintance when were out eating, "good luck with that...you'll never be able to get it done." I wrote a five page letter, which documented specific issues and breakdowns which occurred within the system. Thankfully, my relentless approach enabled me to get the attention of the right people and, most importantly, our mother was able to live in respectful dignity the rest of her years.

Mom had been steadily failing. In the fall of 2004, it had really become noticeable. I'll never forget stopping in to visit and finding her badly leaning over to her left while sitting in an arm chair. She was pretty out of it and drooling somewhat. For the first and only time, I could not stay there very long and Julie knew it. I apologized to Mom and the staff, but I had to leave. In early February of 2005, she'd developed a bed sore which wouldn't heal. I underestimated the seriousness of it and she ended up dying from its complications. She'd been designated for hospice care a couple of days prior to her death.

Julie was able to talk with Mom the night before she passed. I heard her clearly say to Julie, "take care of him." This was quite remarkable at this point because she otherwise seemed non-communicative. It was very obvious that her time here was short. I'd been in frequent contact with Doug and Shirley. We had already pursued funeral related arrangements and had picked out Mom's casket. I called them and told them to be sure to come down early the next day.

In the morning of her passing it was noticeably dreary. This was on Friday, February 11th, 2005. I stopped in to see Mom very early that day; as I needed to set up our display

Gary and his mother at Encore facility.

booth for an annual Home and Garden Show that was to be beginning later that afternoon. I remember it being very cold in the expo hall and a large back door was partially open. Flying around, my mind was pretty cluttered as I was attempting to get everything ready. I hurried to get back to the Alzheimer's facility and Doug and Shirley were already there. I was so thankful that I'd gotten back prior to Mom's passing and had the much appreciated opportunity to be there with my brother and sister-in-law by her side for some precious few hours. Shirley was sitting on her bed and we each held her hand. We told her it was okay to pass and it seemed that she understood. Not long thereafter, she moved on.

I called the funeral home and started things in motion. We discussed the timing of the funeral and determined it would be on the following Tuesday. She'd passed at 1:15. The three of us consoled each other and stayed to visit for awhile. As difficult as it was, none of us wanted to see our Mother suffer any more. She was such a prideful individual and it had reached a point where she no longer had a quality of life. Knowing my Mom, if it would have been her choice she would have left of us earlier. Not because she wanted to leave us, but because she didn't want to see us carrying the incessant strain of trying to help her.

Shortly after leaving the facility I crossed a long bridge on my way back to the expo building. About one-third of the way across the bridge, clouds

honestly opened up to considerable sun. I experienced such a powerful feeling of peace that I've never felt before or since. The best way to describe it was this incredible feeling of comfort washed over me. It definitely grabbed my attention. I believe it was Mom's way of saying everything was fine and that she was finally at peace. With great humility, I now understand....it was THE PEACE THAT PASSETH ALL UNDERSTANDING.

My dear Mom.

⚔ 4 ⚕
NOT THE STEVE ROSE Who...?

It was a late Friday afternoon on February 11, 2005, and I had returned to the Sunnyview Expo Center for the start of an Annual Winnebagoland Home Builders' Association Home and Garden Show. I had the first booth setup in the back center area of the hall, at its far left side. My wife had arrived from her teaching job to help work the booth with me. The very first person to stop by our spot was a gentleman who seemed to be around my age at about 4:45. He looked over our printed list of names of small business customers and mentioned that we knew some people in common. I then asked him his name and he said "my name is Steve Rose." I replied, "not the Steve Rose who worked at WNAM radio in Neenah for many years?" After he answered "that's me", I likely looked like I saw a ghost. I told him that my mother had talked to me several times about him over the years. He asked me her name and seemed as visibly shocked as I was after being told it; he literally jumped back and said, "Your Mother is Grace Beyer!"; Steve said that she was an awesome lady and that he'd definitely like to meet her some time; He said he'd only talked with her over the phone a number of times, but that she'd helped him out a great deal. Steve said back then he'd been going through some difficult times.

I then sadly told him that setting up a meeting with my Mom would no longer be possible at this point, because she had passed away, just earlier that afternoon, at 1:15 p.m. He said he was so sorry to hear this and asked me if I knew when the services would be held, because he wanted to attend them.

I finished my senior year at Neenah High School in June of 1971. My Dad passed away on August 3rd. My mother had certainly proven herself to be someone you could count on in the toughest of circumstances. She had been a willing and dependable caregiver for many different family members over the years; not just my father. They were welcomed in our

Gary with his parents. circa 1971

home and she always exhibited God given strength and mercy.

I started college in September of 1971 and was welcomed to still live at home. My commute was only about 25 minutes and we had a very good relationship. My only brother and sister-in-law lived in the house next door. This was good for both of us. I was still pretty wet behind the ears and my mother sure appreciated my company. Being an accounting major, the homework load was significant. I was also growing up and going out to the bars with friends; especially during my junior and senior years. This became a major stress reliever for me.

I got a job working in a Super Valu grocery store in Neenah beginning in 1972. I started on Wednesday night, February 2nd and this happened to be the same day that numbers were being drawn for a national draft lottery associated with the Vietnam War. I remember listening to a rundown of the numbers on my car radio as I was heading from school to work. I heard my number was 315 and I was ecstatic. With my Dad being gone I knew it was important for me to be around. The numbers were to be called for active service beginning with the next year.

When I graduated in 1975 the job market was tough, but I was offered a nice accounting job in Green Bay. I was to work in the corporate accounting office for a large cheese manufacturing company whose headquarters was located there. My responsibilities were to assist the accounting head for the Logan, Utah, plant. I drove back and forth from my mother's home in Neenah for the first seven months. It reached a point where with my erratic work hours and associated stress I needed to move closer to work.

I got an apartment on the east side of Green Bay and lived there until I resigned from my position in June of 1976. I had been taking a one night per week CPA review class in Appleton, but the Corporate Controller was not very encouraging or supportive of my associated efforts at that time. He'd said I'd likely be needing to work some hours which would conflict with this effort. I ended up quitting this review course only to realize later that the night and time this class was held could have readily been accommodated without any disruption of my work responsibilities. Even the timing of typical month-end tasks made it such that we didn't need to work late on Tuesdays. I moved back home and was able to get a job working in the Student Loans Office at the University. My intention was to start Graduate School in the fall. A year later, I was back working full-time in the world of corporate accounting and taking graduate classes at night.

I ended up taking a job as Assistant Controller for a division of a company that was located in rural Berlin, Wisconsin. Driving back and forth became impractical and I got a nice apartment there near the end of 1978. My mother was a fiercely independent woman and I don't remember her ever complaining about much of anything. With the death of my Dad she found other ways to help pass the time. She was a regular listener to WNAM radio in Neenah. She would call in for various reasons. Many times it was because they were offering some type of promotion or contest.

I distinctly remember her commonly talking about a disc jockey who worked there whose name was Steve Rose. It seemed like they had developed a nice friendship and she regularly spoke highly of him to me. My mother always liked visiting with people and she was well-liked herself. She was known as a relentless worker who always cut her own large lawn and shoveled her own considerable snow. You'd never see my mother dressed sloppily, regardless of what she was doing or where she was going. She was typically in a nice looking dress with high heels. I rarely remember her in slacks until much later in her life.

Steve Rose worked for many years as a DJ on WNAM Radio in Neenah, but

Gary's mother, Grace.

21

I'd never met or talked with him before that memorable afternoon on Friday, February 11, 2005. As promised, he attended my mother's visitation on Tuesday night, February 15th at Konrad-Behlman Funeral Home on the west side of Oshkosh. We've since developed a treasured friendship. Steve told me it was the incident of how and when we met at the Expo Center which gave him the impetus to write his awesome book <u>Coincidence or Godincidence</u>. Steve's written a number of other books including <u>Leap of Faith: God Must Be a Packer Fan</u>, <u>Leap of Faith 2: God Loves Packer Fans</u> and <u>Leap of Faith 3: The Packer Hall of Faith</u>...with the Packers LeRoy Butler, <u>7 Steps from Your Dreams To Your Destiny</u> and <u>Pea Soup For The Packer Heart</u>. He is also a very highly respected motivational speaker.

The wonderful story behind Steve's book <u>Coincidence or Godincidence</u> continues to evolve. It is hard to believe that it's 2013 and over eight years since my mother's passing. Thanks to his considerable efforts, the basis of this book is gaining more and more recognition. Soon it will likely begin some momentum on a national level with the support of Johnsonville Foods. A Premiere showing regarding the book's stories took place in Appleton on Wednesday night, September 18th at their impressive Performing Arts Center. Starting on Sunday night, September 29th, television stations in five different Wisconsin cities debuted a thirty minute weekly television series based on this book.

As Steve would say...there are no coincidences, there are only Godincidences. It was clearly a Godincidence for he and I to finally meet, in the way we did, on the very same day that my mother Grace had passed. Yes, it was THE STEVE ROSE WHO my mother had specifically spoken so highly of over the years. It's extremely interesting when I reflect on how our own lives became spiritually intertwined.

✺ 5 ✺
YOUR ONLY BROTHER
and You Weren't Even...

...invited to his wedding; it's only because I hadn't been born yet. Doug used to always tell people that we were 24 years apart in age. I'd always quickly counter that the difference was only 23-1/2 years. Growing up, this was a bit awkward because others would tell my parents that they "had their own grandchild" or that "Doug and Shirley could have been his parents". The facts were that I proudly had only one set of parents and one brother and sister-in-law; unfortunately, a sister, whose name was Charmaine, had passed away well before I was born.

Doug and Shirley got married on August 25, 1951, and I was born in June of 1953. I couldn't celebrate their wedding day with them, but made sure I was able to help them celebrate both their 25th and their 50th anniversaries in style.

Back in the late 40s and early 50s, big band music was going strong. My brother always loved music and was an outstanding dancer. He liked to visit the dance halls located in the Fox River Valley with friends. This one Sunday evening at the Nightengale Ballroom on the outskirts of the city of Kaukauna, Wisconsin he was attracted to this girl who he first saw standing against a railing there. He got the courage up and approached her. He asked her name and invited her out on the floor for a dance.

They danced a few songs and went their separate ways. Shirley said that she didn't see much of him the rest of the evening. This was a two-floor facility with a nice bar in its lower level. She had taken the bus there from her home in nearby Little Chute. Doug had driven there that evening with two friends. He was pretty smitten with this girl whose name was Shirley Van Asten. As the evening was drawing more to a close, he went back to talk with Shirley. He asked her if he could give her a ride home and she was aware that he'd come there with two other friends. She obviously was somewhat attracted to him, as well, because she told him yes.

Doug & Shirley with baby Gary.

The two friends sat in the backseat and Doug walked Shirley to the back door of her parents home. He told her that he appreciated meeting her. In the meantime, his friends proceeded to play with the spot lights that were attached to his car. This caused him to hasten the conversation, but before he left that evening he looked directly at Shirley and told her, "I'm going to marry you." You can imagine how she must have felt.

They began dating regularly and clearly hit it off. Shirley was just graduating from high school in 1950, and my brother had graduated in 1948. He worked in the plant at Neenah Foundry Company. Like many young couples, they had their disagreements and their ups and downs, but when my brother died in September of 2006 they were able to say that they were recently married for a total of 55 years.

On February 9, 1955, they won a large dance contest featuring the Ralph Flanagan Orchestra. They received a gorgeous personalized trophy which is still proudly displayed in Shirley's curio cabinet. When they took the floor to dance, people would consistently turn their attention to them. Watching them jitterbug was always a real treat. As others said, "nobody does it better." They just loved to dance and that became very obvious over the years.

My brother was an excellent drummer and he played in a small two to three piece combo band for a number of years. His primary partner, Frank, played the Hammond organ and they were called The Tempo Tones. They would contract to play weddings and both private and public parties throughout the area. Their reputation was strong and so was their following. The engagements were normally on Friday and Saturday nights. They were even booked during the summertime to play at some Northern campground bars.

Our Dad died in early August of 1971. Doug and Dad worked at the same company for many years. Doug possessed a tremendous, God given art talent. He could sit down and draw almost anything at anytime. He also did extremely well in drafting class in high school and had the ability to visualize and draw out complex structures and accurately synchronize them to scale. Some of his work was just fabulous. He should have been an architect because he would have made a very good one. When Doug was in his mid-teens, he carved a horse out of wood that would highly impress even the most talented of wood carvers. After he and Shirley were married he tackled the carving of a larger horse out of a block of walnut. These are exquisite works of art and I have one of them proudly displayed in our home. His talents didn't go unnoticed by the foundry, but they were significantly squandered in the scope of his work responsibilities there. He designed their NF logo that was used on all of their trucks and catalogs.

His position was eliminated after 28 years in 1973. He didn't go on to a college or trade school after finishing high school. He was busy helping my father and mother build their custom home for over five long years after working full time at the foundry. The house was finished in 1955. My parents gave Doug and Shirley a piece of land next to their home where they would have their own home built. His considerable art and associated design talents were under utilized within his work environment. Fortunately, he was able to take advantage of them in his personal life.

Doug put his creative skills to use wherever possible. In the basement of their home he designed and built an impressive floor to ceiling stone fireplace which was beautifully curved as it headed back towards the fire pit area. He took an evening class at the technical school in town to learn how to use their wood lathes to turn large, decorative spindles for placement around his basement bar. He designed a dramatic back wall for their dining room carved out of wood. His architectural skills were used to design a gorgeous second floor addition to our parents home which would overcome the major problems associated with what had become a troublesome flat top roof.

Later, his incredible talents enabled him to visualize, re-design and completely draw to scale some major modifications to their small cottage in North Central Wisconsin. This involved an actual shift of the existing building from its foundation, recognizing and ordering appropriate building-related materials and acting as the general contractor for the entire project. He actually took his detailed blueprints and related drawings to an architect for reinforcement and confirmation of his work. The architect was blown away by them. Prior to this, he had designed a large, two-story barn to be built on this same property. The intensive level of work involved with each of these efforts took place over considerable periods of time. In hindsight, they were

Doug and Shirley's 50th anniversary celebration.

both cathartic in nature. This gave my brother a sense of pride after excelling at these remarkable accomplishments. Impressively meeting these challenges clearly boosted his self esteem and were invaluable for strengthening his own self image during a very difficult period in his life.

Thankfully, I was able to celebrate their 25th wedding anniversary with them in August of 1976. I played the drums during that memorable evening with my brother's former band partner playing the organ. Then, Julie and I were able to plan their 50th anniversary celebration in 2001. We sure had fun. Initially, they weren't real excited about having a large celebration, but thankfully we were able to convince them to do so and they were glad that they did. It was held at the same place where our wedding reception took place 13 years earlier. It featured the same band too; they were named Just The Two Of Us. What was really neat is that they were able to locate and have the priest who married them attend. It was extremely difficult, but I was finally able to get our Mom to leave the dementia facility for awhile so she could be there. This was very important to all of us and she sure seemed to enjoy herself once she got to their celebration. I recorded this very special event using a camcorder and we had the results transferred over to disk copies for each of us to enjoy.

Doug was MY ONLY BROTHER, but I'll never forget him. He had a childlike enthusiasm for life and always seemed to appreciate the little things. He loved his brother too and I know he was very proud of me. I learned a lot from him and we became closer as I got older. I miss him a lot these days and would love to have the opportunity to ask for his advice from time to time. I know he's helping us too. He and Shirley were blessed to have a wonderful marriage and yes, I did get to celebrate their marriage with them during a larger scale celebration. It just occurred a number of years later and thankfully, this was able to happen not only once, but twice.

Gary at Doug & Shirley's 25th Wedding Anniversary celebration in 1976.

༪ 6 ༫
"WAT YOU THINK MON?"
(Followed By a Brief Pause, Then)
"MAYBE SHOOT 'EM IN DA HEAD?"

My friend Paul and I visited our buddy Gary when he was teaching in St. Thomas of the U.S. Virgin Islands in the spring of 1985. He picked us up at the small airport there and took us back to his place in the hills in an open-top jeep. I had never been outside the continental United States before. The weather was absolutely perfect and he made us refreshing pina coladas right after we got inside. We had an awesome time in the week we were there. Late during the night before I was to leave, I was awakened by some noise that was coming from outside the small window with vertical bars that was above my right shoulder. I normally was a very sound sleeper.

Shortly thereafter, I heard the comments referenced in the heading above from two, softer sounding voices; I was most definitely awake at that point and this scared the bejeebers out of me. I kept my eyes closed and tried to stay as motionless as possible (I honestly had thoughts of President Kennedy's assassination passing quickly through my mind). After what seemed like an eternity to me, but was probably just five minutes or so, I quietly whispered to Paul, "did you hear that?" and woke him up. At this point, a dog was barking loudly outside and Paul annoyingly said, "it's only a dog" and I said, "yeah…now!"

Paul had first met Gary in a college Spanish class and later, we all became very good friends. He was from the town of Chilton, Wisconsin, and became recognized as an adopted member of "the Neenah Boys." We each took our college years seriously, but we enjoyed having some fun along the way too. Paul and I did not live on or near campus. We commuted the 15 or so miles from our hometown of Neenah. Three of us high school friends took turns driving in weekly blocks during our junior and senior years; Paul had transferred to the University of Wisconsin-Oshkosh from another state school starting with his junior year. Our other friend Randy

Gary, myself and Paul in St. Thomas in 1985.

had intentions of becoming an optometrist and has not only been a long-time friend of ours, but he's also Paul's and my eye doctor (as he is for each of our wives).

This was back in a time when the drinking age in Wisconsin was 18. By the time we each hit our junior years we were enjoying the campus bars on Friday and Saturday nights. Thursday night was also big; especially for those students who commonly headed back to their hometowns for the weekend. Our favorite meeting spot was at a bar named Toshs. It was as basic a place as it gets, but the environment was fun and the music on the jukebox there was exceptional. At the time it provided a comfortable setting to relieve some stress. By the time Gary Ludwig reached his junior year, he and three other friends from back home were living together in off-campus housing. They were sharing the rent associated with an older, two-story house. It was only about a block from campus and just a couple of blocks from the college bars. He always called it "the crony estate" and I thought it was because he lived with some so-called cronies from Chilton. It turned out that the owner's last name was actually Krohn.

I'll tell you what...there were a lot of good times which were associated with that place. My Dad had passed away late in the summer before I started college. I welcomed the camaraderie that we all shared. I was growing up during this time; as we all were. The stress associated with the upper level accounting courses was pleasantly and significantly offset by the many good times we shared together.

Gary was working towards his undergraduate and later graduate degrees in counseling. Randy moved on towards his pursuit of graduate and doctorate degrees in optometry in the state of Illinois. Paul and I proceeded to work full-time. After about a year, I quit my first accounting job in Green Bay with the intention of pursuing my MBA at UW-Oshkosh on a full-time basis. I was able to find a part-time job on campus as a graduate assistant in the accounting office, working in the student loans area. I worked there from July of 1976 to March of 1977. The pay was pretty low and I was hungry to get back to working full-time in the corporate accounting world.

I continued to take graduate classes in the evening and completed my MBA in finance and accounting in 1980.

I'd called off a planned wedding in February of 1981. Thanks to the support of friends like Paul, Randy and Gary, I'd gotten my head in good shape and was pretty entrenched in an every day, work comes first mindset. The timing of our trip to St. Thomas in March of 1985 was perfect for Paul and myself. Gary had gotten a teaching job there and invited us to come for a visit. I had quit my job with Wells Manufacturing in mid-March after accepting a job offer with Morgan Products Ltd. I was being paid for earned vacation through the end of March and was to be beginning my new position near the start of April. We were each looking forward to a much needed getaway and the opportunity to spend some quality time with a good friend.

Gary and another teacher, whose name is Bill, were sharing the rent for part of a residence that was located in the hillside of Bolongo Bay. The property was owned by a lady whose business was associated with interior decorating and design. It was secured with fencing that was normally locked and she also had a formidable German Shepherd around for protection. Gary had teaching responsibilities during the day when we were there, but he'd given us outstanding advice and Paul and I made the most of our time. He also had a part-time job at the Frenchman's Reef Hotel that was near Bolongo Bay. As time would permit, Gary and Bill would commonly join us. Thankfully, we were there over a weekend and their availability increased. We were able to take boat tours to the islands of St. John's and Virgin Gorda in the British Virgin Islands. The La Bomba Charger and La Bomba Challenger will always be remembered fondly. Virgin Gorda was literally an island paradise. The Reef's Bay hike we took was exceptional.

We spent time on the beach at Magen's Bay and on Coki's Beach by St. Thomas' Coral World. The Virgin Grand Resort Hotel was very impressive. We also visited the Sapphire Bay Beach Resort there. During our stay we were able to consistently enjoy some magnificent sunsets. The memorable Charlotte Amalie Harbor was a focal point of the island. St. Thomas offers wonderful views of both the Atlantic Ocean and the Caribbean Sea.

Gary and Bill graciously shared their small bedroom with us. They split apart the two beds into separate box springs and mattresses. There was a small dresser against the wall that was near where the window was located. Paul and

I bought a few things while we were there and I remember leaving my new gold band watch on this dresser before I laid down to sleep each night. I'd fallen for this tall wooden statue of attention-getting "Fitu LeFanc." My flights home with Fitu, as a carry on, would make for a good story all by itself.

As I said earlier, I normally was a very sound sleeper. I was definitely awake when I heard the comments that came from outside the window. Gary had also woke up after I'd awakened Paul and we then talked a bit more. He said the owner would let her German Shepherd guard dog run loose in the fenced in yard. However, he said that it definitely was not typical for it to be barking like it was at the time. I needed to leave a day earlier than Paul and nothing was apparently wrong after we'd gotten up the next morning. Gary later told us that the day after Paul had left…there was a shooting nearby. There also was a forced break-in of their residence shortly after we'd left for home. Gary said that the landlady had recently been moving larger pieces of furniture to act as a blockade to the entry of the residence.

Something was clearly awry during the timeframe we'd spent there. No one could have gotten in through the bedroom window, but a gun could have been shot in the spacing between the vertical bars (if only to frighten). About a month after we'd left, Gary was shot at while delivering furniture for the landlady while driving her van. He said he was driving down Waterfront Street when he heard a thud. He pulled over and found a bullet hole in the back of the van. He saw that a bullet had lodged in a board of a crate that was helping to protect the furniture.

A lesson learned here is to recognize how quickly one's perspective can change on a particular experience in their life. We had a pretty carefree and enjoyable time during the week we were able to spend together in this

tropical paradise. The pleasant memories will live with us forever. However, I'll also never forget how truly scared I was for that relatively short time period during the night before I was to be leaving for home. Life is precious and we should never take it for granted.

Gary ended up being recognized as "Teacher Of The Year" on the island of St. Thomas for 1985. WAT YOU THINK MON? This couldn't have happened to a more deserving person.

Gary with Mrs Jones.

CAN YOU BELIEVE IT, My Mother Wants My Cousin Laura...?

...to be my Maid of Honor. I'll never forget this comment, which my fiancee Bonnie made to me not long after we'd gotten engaged in June of 1980. I told her that this decision was, and strictly should be, up to her. She adamantly said that she wanted my sister-in-law, Shirley, to fill the Matron of Honor role in our wedding. Bonnie told me that she wasn't even that close to her cousin Laura.

We were first introduced solely because of Shirley's thoughtfulness and level of mutual consideration for the two of us. This matter was complicated by the fact that she was also Bonnie's immediate boss at Kimberly Clark Corporation. This was not something that Shirley would normally get involved with and she definitely was more than a bit uncomfortable doing so.

Being born later in my parents' lives impacted the dynamics of my childhood. I had two very proud and responsible parents as well as a brother and sister-in-law living right next door, who were nearly as proud and were old enough to be my parents. There was a lot of love going around and I didn't lack for much. I never once felt the least bit short-changed by having parents who were much older than me.

My Dad's health issues were difficult to watch because he was such an awesome guy. My mother consistently displayed an unforgettable level of strength and courage throughout her entire life. I couldn't help but become more and more impressed as the years went on and I came closer to becoming an adult.

I never dated in high school. I never went to a prom or a homecoming dance. This is not intended to be sour grapes. Rather, it was a period in my life where I needed to spend considerable time in a hospital and at home, much less obviously, encouraging my parents as they were encouraging me. My priorities were different than they are for most kids during this time and

I never attempted to go out for any sports. I was ready for college and the entire experience was good for me. The fall of my freshman year I attended a handful of my old high school's football games. There was a cheerleader on their squad whose name was Debbie. She was a year younger than me ,and I had a crush on her in my last year of high school; she didn't know it though.

After one of the games, I was able to get the courage up to go over and attempt to talk with her. To my surprise, she seemed receptive to me and I asked her out on a date. We dated a number of times and I really got to like her. She was planning on going to Carthage College in Kenosha. She had the cutest baby brother; who, ironically, was also born later in life. I would be sure to walk her to her parents' front door, but couldn't muster the courage to give her a kiss good night. This went on for awhile and had reached a point where I would go home and bury my head in my pillow in frustration. Finally, this got addressed. I embarrassingly brought it up and I'll never forget what she said to me. "At first, I thought you were just shy. Then later, I thought maybe you just didn't want to," was her feedback. I was so ashamed of myself and we never dated again after having this conversation.

I didn't date much when I was an undergraduate in college either. Close friends and I enjoyed going to the bars on the weekends, especially during my junior and senior years. The last thing I wanted at the time was a serious relationship. I was much too busy with my first priority of earning my accounting degree. After this time, I was to become more interested in the pursuit of an ongoing relationship. I even joined an area singles club for awhile. I met some very nice women but none of them caused me to consider settling down. I brought a girl that I'd been dating to my brother and sister-in-law's 25th wedding anniversary celebration. She was certainly ready to talk about the possibility of getting married, but I wasn't.

It's a compliment when friends, family and co-workers are trying to match you up with someone. It also can be a bit awkward. My first boss out of college and his wife were concerned with this. After attending a company Christmas party in Green Bay I was offered to stay overnight at a female co-worker's place. I hadn't moved there yet and was planning on driving the 50-mile trek back home. Word sure got around and it was all completely innocent. My boss and his wife, when I worked at Medalist, arranged an evening "get acquainted" dinner at their home for such a purpose. Later, Shirley helped set the wheels in motion for me to meet a co-worker of hers from from a department that she worked closely with. We basically met on a blind date and went out for quite some time. I was planning to break things off when I got involved in a very serious car accident. Things became all the more difficult because she really cared for me and would regularly spend considerable time with me at the hospital. She was also there for me as I was recuperating, and later when I returned to work. I just didn't have the same level of feelings for her that she apparently had for me. I've never been one to string anyone along in relationships and I usually made myself out to being the bad guy. There were times I would just stop calling because I believed that there was no good way to end things without hurting the other person's feelings.

Bonnie and I ended up meeting each other at the Chalice Restaurant in Oshkosh for a date. We had talked on the telephone a couple of times and had seen pictures of each other prior to this taking place. She was an only child who still lived at home; I was impressed by the fact that she'd been taking flying lessons and must, therefore, be pretty independent. We definitely hit it off right away. She was cute and had an upbeat personality. She also seemed to have a zest for life and these were some of the important things I was looking for in a potential partner.

She and her parents lived in a very secluded home on the outskirts of my home town of Neenah. Her mother was a homemaker and her father worked in maintenance at the same company where Bonnie worked in a customer service capacity. They owned a small cabin in Northern Wisconsin and developed a habit of going up there most weekends, especially during the summer time. They were accustomed to taking Bonnie along. They were very protective of her. She hadn't learned to cook and her mother would regularly do her laundry. They took a major vacation every year and this typically involved international travel. Bonnie's way was always paid for and they went to Greece late in the summer we'd gotten engaged. I was not invited. All they seemed to prefer in their lives was a routine existence that included their daughter being in a prominent role.

We quickly began to enjoy each other's company and were exclusively dating at least once a week. However, we commonly saw each other three times a week. She was a smoker and told me she was going to quit; she said her parents didn't know about it. Well, they weren't stupid and they likely smelt it on her clothes, regardless of how hard she tried to hide it from them. This bothered me and I told her that I wanted her to quit. I had come to the conclusion that still living with her parents was causing her considerable stress and that our relationship was badly suffering because of this fact. I incorrectly believed that once we got married, things would improve dramatically. I thought she would quit smoking, become more stable and not want to escape as frequently to bar-like environments.

Needless to say, Shirley and my brother Doug were both highly honored and extremely proud when they were asked to be their younger brother's most featured attendants for his wedding. The matter of her cousin Laura being her Maid of Honor seemed like a non-issue. Bonnie planned on honoring her mother by wearing her wedding dress. She told me that she'd talked with her about it and had even tried it on. She said that it did not require any alterations to be made, but that it was to be professionally dry cleaned.

We had our significant issues that would crop up. Bonnie told me that she'd been engaged once before. It became more and more evident to both of us that her parents would prefer it if we were to break up. They kept pushing for me to sign a pre-nuptial agreement prior to our wedding. She owned a small, older home which was used strictly as rental property. I even agreed to attend a meeting between the three of them and their lawyer. I was definitely not interested in signing any type of pre-nup arrangement. I had a lot more to lose than she did and I viewed this as a built-in divorce clause within our marriage. Her parents liked my mother and so did Bonnie during most of our time together. However, I was also presented with the issue that she'd changed her mind and wanted to keep her maiden name. Not even hyphenated, mind you, but she did not want to incorporate the name Beyer in her last name. My Dad means a ton to me and this was a major slap in my face. These were a couple of irreconcilable issues for me. I'm convinced that her parents believed this would finally break us up.

Shirley was diagnosed with female cancer in the summer of 1980. She was always a trooper, and I'd like to believe that the opportunity to be the Matron of Honor in her only brother-in-law's wedding kept her highly driven to successfully overcome this obstacle. She continued to show steady progress in her recovery from major surgery and it was clear that she was aiming at still being able to stand up in our wedding. She's a special lady; who's quietly very sincere and well-meaning. Bonnie liked her as a boss and would say stuff like, "who else but Shirley should be my Matron of Honor." Her mother, however, wanted a family member in that role.

Doug, Shirley and Bonnie.

Bonnie and I "jointly" purchased an older, two-story home on the north side of Oshkosh. Like myself, she wasn't interested in renting at this stage. I was living and working in Berlin when we first met. This is about 25 miles west of Oshkosh. We looked at a number of homes together; each of which was consciously located in Oshkosh. She was working and living about 15 miles north. We'd each have to drive about the same distance to work. I also wanted her parents to know that she'd put some of her own money down towards our purchase of this home. Her contribution was one thousand dollars, but her formal commitment represented even more. She told me that her parents strictly forbid her from moving into the home prior to our wedding. I respected that. The problem was that she was not even to spend a night there, at least as far as her parents knew. It always seemed that she was attempting to satisfy the wishes of her parents; yet she was very effective at playing both ends to the middle while telling me the things I wanted to hear as well.

Our wedding was to be on Valentine's Day 1981. Many times Bonnie would communicate her resolve to making our relationship work. She would regularly say things like I can hardly wait until we're finally married. Things will get much better. I was no longer quite so sure. Just about a month before the scheduled wedding there was that memorable Friday evening we spent in Green Bay. I picked her up after work and we actually had a very nice evening; we were relaxing while having some drinks sitting at a bar. Before leaving, alcohol had taken its toll and a bomb was dropped. She said, "we're not going to be getting married unless you agree to sign a pre-nup." She said her parents were insisting on this. I said, "who's supposed to be getting married?" I was fuming and here she's sleeping in the car all the way home. Bonnie definitely had a drinking problem and it would flare up mercilessly from time to time. As anyone knows who's ever dealt with this type of over-riding issue, time is the only thing which allows the people impacted by this to get beyond it. She would forget things that she'd done and said and it was like they never took place.

Other troublesome issues had been building up and our wedding was truly in serious jeopardy. One evening, two very concerned friends of mine stopped over to the house to talk to with me about it. In fact about ten days or so before the wedding, I stopped to check on how much money I'd lose if I was to cancel the two-week Jamaican honeymoon cruise that I had paid for. It was scheduled to leave one week after our wedding concluded. We were both going in to work that first week.

If you're ever confronted with a similar circumstance I recommend that you do not take this type of comment with a grain of salt. Anything that starts with, "CAN YOU BELIEVE IT?....is worth giving your utmost attention.

∞ 8 ∞
The Grace Of God Gave Us
NEARLY ANOTHER 18 MONTHS

Health-related issues surface in our lives from time to time. They may be our own; they may be of family members that are close to us or they may be of other people that we care very much for. Our level of concern seems to be dependent on a few different things. These are commonly as follows, and they're not intended to be prioritized: the degree of pain involved and what it seems to be emanating from, the type of associated illness, disease or infliction, the level of impact it's having on your/their daily lives and the age of the person being impacted.

I've learned that it's best to be proactive in such matters, but, unfortunately, there are times when this is not possible. The issues needing to be dealt with can be sudden or they can be caused over a period of time. The point is that they should not and many times, cannot afford to be merely ignored.

Many of us have experienced bloating issues from time to time. It's usually uncomfortable and unsightly in appearance. We get frustrated and somewhat concerned, but it's typically not a cause for alarm. I seem to be bothered with digestion-related issues and as I've gotten older, they've become more apparent. A big factor is our loss of enzymes in the digestive process as we age. I've become a huge believer in supplementation since being diagnosed with the muscle disease in January of 2008. Prior to this, I rarely even took vitamins and considered myself to be pretty healthy.

My brother Doug had surgery for prostate cancer in February of 1994. It was a long surgery and when the doctor talked with us, he said that he was concerned that the cancer may have spread and suggested we err on the side of caution. His prostate gland was removed and Doug was given monthly Lupron shots for a number of years. After these shots, he was significantly weakened for the subsequent three days. They really hit him hard. As time went on, he continued to test well and we had periodic

Doug, the architect at work.

conversations regarding the need to continue getting these shots. It was tempting to stop them, but he never did. We thought it best that he still should err on the side of caution.

He had some other health issues and was on considerable medication over the years. I will never forget sitting down to eat with him and he'd pull out this plastic pill bottle. There must have been a dozen or more pills he'd need to take typically prior to or during his meals. He was religious about taking them too. He was following what he was told to do by his doctors.

Doug always had a child-like enthusiasm and maintained a zest for life. He figured it out a lot earlier than I have. It took awhile, as it does with most of us, but in his later years he was way ahead of most people. He always appreciated trees and the inherent beauty of nature…well before I did in my life, but his love for simple things clearly grew as he got older. He'd been in the middle of various corporate battles over his 28 years in the foundry business. He'd become battle fatigued and did his best to keep me in check with my own challenges. As with many of us, though, that was often easier said than done. We can all be thick-headed from time to time. He wanted me to learn from some of his mistakes,

Doug and Shirley's original cottage.

but our own circumstances are always different, right?

I remember my brother being pretty intense when I was growing up. He could be volatile and prone to a quick temper. He'd stand up for what he believed was right and was assertive, but his intentions were good. He didn't like seeing his little

Doug and Shirley's remodeled cottage.

brother get hurt. When his position was eliminated in March of 1973, it was hard on him. He didn't have a college degree or a trade to fall back on. His talents were considerable, but he'd not been able to take enough advantage of them in his various positions at the foundry. The suitable opportunities just were not there.

His considerable architectural and design talents enabled him to visualize, re-design and draw to scale some extensive modifications to their small cottage in North Central Wisconsin. This project involved a shift of the existing building from its foundation, recognizing and ordering appropriate building-related materials and acting as the general contractor for the endeavor. It turned out magnificently. His detailed blueprints were as accurate as one could have and the sub-contractors were thoroughly impressed. He'd previously designed and drew the blueprints for a large, two-story barn on this same property. It was not your typical barn either. There were cantilevered windows and a large, impressive deck off the back of the second floor. Doug missed his true calling. He likely would have been a been a sought-after architect in our area.

I'll never forget stopping over at Doug and Shirley's house one late afternoon. He was sitting in a chair in their living room. Shirley was upset with him that his clothes weren't fitting him. Many of us have been faced with this from time to time. I told him good luck with it and that I'd been frustrated with bloating episodes. Well, these weren't comparable bloating episodes. Things weren't getting better in this regard and he addressed this with his doctor. Testing revealed that he had a major liver-related problem. He was not a candidate for a transplant with his combined age and diabetic issues. The latter had gotten worse, as well, and he had been on insulin for awhile. In the past, he was, what was referred to as, a diet-controlled diabetic.

He was diagnosed with cirrhosis of the liver. The considerable interactions associated with excessive medication over the years were destroying his liver. He wasn't ever a teetotaler, but certainly was not a heavy drinker either. He was in and out of the hospital and needed numerous liver-associated paracentesis procedures to be done. This involved insertion of a long needle to help drain the considerable build up of fluid in his abdomen. I couldn't believe the amount that was removed during each of the respective procedures. It had become, what seemed to be, a lost cause.

Our mother died two weeks short of her ninety third birthday; she passed away three days prior to Valentine's Day in February of 2005. At the same time, Doug was clearly fighting a major uphill battle. We were honestly not sure if he was even going to be able to attend Mom's funeral. He was heavily jaundiced. I'll never forget going with Shirley and Doug to the funeral home to discuss arrangements for our mother's service, etc. Afterwards, we stopped to eat at Jansen's Restaurant. It was a very sunny day and as we were about to walk inside, I really detected the degree of jaundicing that was in his face. He was such a trooper, but clearly was very weak. He usually had a pretty good appetite, but not on this day. He'd ordered a cup of soup and a sandwich and couldn't even finish eating his soup. This was really hard on me. Here, my mother was dying and my only was brother didn't seem to be too far behind her.

It was Tuesday evening, February 15th. We live very near the funeral home and Doug and Shirley stopped by our house first so we could head over there together. I'll never forget it. I felt so sorry for him throughout the visitation; you could tell that everyone else there did as well. I was focused on giving Mom her due respect and honor during this very difficult evening. Doug was so weak and had a very difficult time standing, let alone walking. He was visibly draining from the paracentesis that was done that same afternoon. Visitors at the funeral said that he actually looked worse than Mom did inside the casket. I did not know where to turn, but just tried to carry on and get through that evening. Mom was dressed in the beautiful pink dress that she wore at our wedding. Considering her age, there was a surprisingly large turnout at the funeral home (and the visitors included Steve Rose; as he'd promised Julie and I at the Expo four days earlier). I was an emotional wreck inside, but I knew that it was extremely important for me to stay strong. The last thing my brother or Shirley needed was for me to lose it.

Gary and his brother Doug.

Doug was not able to attend the burial services the next day. We sure didn't expect him to either. My brother could have passed away during the same timeframe as our mother had, but thankfully, this wasn't to be his time. This would have been absolutely devastating for our very small family. He experienced a significant bounce back period from the level he was at during the period of the funeral. We were humbly able to enjoy and appreciate his company for quite awhile longer. We all became so very proud of his considerable strength and courage. Julie and I had gotten him a small crystal cross that he so treasured during his difficult times.

He'd been released from the hospital in Appleton when they realized that his time was likely very short and that there was nothing else they could do for him. He was heavily medicated and needed constant oxygen. On Thursday evening, September 21st, 2006, it was apparent that he didn't have much longer to live. We played some videos of happier times in his life and he smiled and clearly appreciated watching them. He realized his time was short and he was so gracious and comfortable with where his faith was going to take him. It was at about 7:00 that evening that he distinctly said to Julie, "you take care of my little bro, you take care of Gary." Julie and I held his hand, kissed him and said our goodbyes. He later passed the next morning at 3:00 a.m. It was Friday morning, September 22nd. He was able to die in his own home with his cherished wife Shirley right near his side.

Thankfully, he and my wonderful and extremely dedicated sister-in-law were able to get some important matters resolved prior to his passing, including the selling of their lakefront property. Doug showed us all so very much. Like my father before him, he left our world with class and dignity. We will always deeply appreciate the fact that the GRACE OF GOD GAVE US NEARLY ANOTHER EIGHTEEN MONTHS to spend with him. This was incredible! He always kept his zest for life, but it's how he handled his frequently overwhelming health issues that will always be inspirational to me and to any others who saw it.

Doug and Shirley.

ೞ 9 ಖ
FRIDAY The 13th, FOLLOWED BY VALENTINE'S DAY

Each year there is one day on the calendar which is recognized as a day to express our feelings of love and caring for the very special people in our lives. This is normally directed towards a spouse, a boy friend or girl friend, parents, grandparents and other special some ones. Regardless of who the intended recipient is, the message is normally one of sincerity.

When Bonnie and I selected Valentine's Day 1981 for our wedding day, I fully intended to make a commitment to a special woman in my life; that went beyond my expression of love for her. I planned on getting married with the belief and expectation that we'd spend the rest of our lives together as husband and wife. You may call me pretty old-fashioned or possibly naive, but I anticipated nothing less.

Prior to dating Bonnie in late 1979, I had never come close to having a serious relationship. I dated some other women, but my primary focus was on getting through college, as soon as possible, and earning my accounting degree. After I finished my undergraduate schooling, I was excited to get into the workforce and finally start earning a desirable income. While I was still in a 'studying mindset' I signed up for an evening CPA review course which was being conducted about 30 miles from where I was working. I believe I went to about three or four of these, once per week, sessions when the Corporate Controller told me it might be best if I waited on this for awhile. He thought my work demands could become conflicting.

I never did attempt to sit for the CPA exam and turned my attention towards getting a master's degree in accounting and finance. My class load was identified as such that it became feasible for me to attempt to do this. I had resigned from my job in Green Bay and was taking multiple classes during the evening while working part-time on campus. It didn't take long for me to get my fill of this because I was used to making a good income for the time

Gary and Bonnie.

and the on campus accounting job paid minimum wage. Being a full-time graduate student was not for me.

By October of 1978, I had accepted an interesting and enjoyable accounting job in the small city of Berlin, Wisconsin. It paid pretty well and I re-located to a nice apartment there. I had been living with my mother since quitting the job that I'd gotten prior to graduating. After recovering from the car accident, I needed to find a different place to live because I'd given up the apartment I had been living in. Thankfully, I was able to find a nice place in a trailer park that wasn't too far from work. The rent was very reasonable and it was actually pretty cozy. I was dating a woman prior to and after the accident, but I knew that I needed to break things off. She was a very nice person, but I did not have an interest in taking the relationship much further.

When Bonnie and I first met, we hit it off quite well. I found her to be interesting and enjoyable to be with. She had a responsible office job, working for my sister-in-law, and had been working there for awhile. Her track record seemed pretty solid and she came across as sensible, fun-loving and intelligent, in no intended order. She was cute and a bit spunky. I understood her to be reasonably self-confident, but not cocky. Bonnie was down-to-earth and this was also very very important to me.

Throughout our dating there were always considerable strains associated with her living with her parents. Being an only child likely didn't help matters, but the issues seemed much bigger than this alone. Upon getting engaged in the summer of 1980, we were both very excited about getting married to each other. This was not only a formal means of confirming our intentions, but it should have done so for others as well. We were both hoping that her parents would back off from their apparent efforts to split us up. Finally, I was even invited to join the three of them for some weekends spent at their cabin in Northern Wisconsin. Bonnie and I would commonly drive up there separately and would then go out around the area in the evening.

In the fall of 1980, things were going along pretty well We joined a couples bowling league in Neenah and teamed with another couple. Bonnie worked with Sue and she and I had gone to high school together. Her husband Steve and I were huge Brewers baseball fans. We bowled every other Saturday evening. Sue was good for Bonnie and she actually had become a great sounding board for her. She even asked her to be one of her bridesmaids in our wedding. Sue was surprised, but accepted. There were to be four pairs of groomsmen and bridesmaids in addition to Doug and Shirley. Sue called me a couple of weeks prior to our wedding and told me that she was strongly considering backing out from being a bridesmaid. Unfortunately, I was only able to fully understand why a bit later.

We had decided to look for a house to buy in Oshkosh. Our intentions were to identify a nice starter-type home. She'd communicated this desire to her parents and they seemed to be supportive, as far as I could tell. I asked her to put some of her own money into the down payment. I thought this would prove to her parents that our wedding was likely going to happen. We found an older, two-story home on the north side of Oshkosh. I was to live there alone until we got married. I was okay with that. Bonnie was very excited about purchasing "our home." You would have thought that periodically she'd want to bring her own car to spend some time with me there, but I was always the driver during our relationship. Ironically, before we met, she had been driving to Oshkosh for weekly flying lessons. She'd take her car to work and a few other places, but that was it.

Too much of our time was spent in bar-like environments. For a time it provided a comfortable escape for both of us from the different stresses going on in our lives. I was busy with work; she was coping with the daily conflicts associated with living at home. The bars were a place that we could relax and have some fun. What became obvious though was that Bonnie had a drinking problem. She was not that big of a person and she loved her Brandy Manhattans. I would consciously drink my drinks slower and slower, but this did not matter. When she was ready for another drink, she'd get another drink. We'd have some very enjoyable times that would get overshadowed by excessive alcohol. Many a time, I drove back home shaking my head and wondering what to do about this. Invariably, the next time we'd talk or see each other she'd have forgotten about what had happened the time before. The apologies were commonly shallow because she didn't know what she was apologizing for.

My sister-in-law Shirley was in the process of successfully recovering from surgery for female cancer. This was detected after our engagement and she was so driven to participate as the Matron of Honor in our wedding. Thankfully, it looked like she was going to be able to do so. Bonnie's mother had wanted her to choose her cousin Laura to be her featured attendant in our wedding. I believed that this matter was closed and was a non-issue.

Bonnie absolutely loved the song "The Rose" by Bette Midler. She couldn't get enough of it and wanted it to be her "walk up the aisle song" for the start of our wedding. The final lyrics of this song are, "in the spring becomes the rose." She often compared herself to becoming that rose on our wedding day. Bonnie was a sentimentalist, as am I, and she planned on wearing her mother's wedding dress. The bridesmaids dresses were to be a complementary shade of red. She had selected the wedding cake and we expected to invite over two hundred people. We'd decided on a two-week Caribbean cruise for our honeymoon. This was to include a one-week's stay in Jamaica. Considerable plans had been made and we were excited about getting married and moving forward with our lives together.

She and her mother were of the Catholic faith. We had reached the point in our relationship where we agreed to attend an evening 'marriage preparation-type' class with Father Michael O'Rourke from her church in my home town of Neenah. This class was to meet once each week for about eight weeks. Bonnie was expected to attend this church, along with her mother, every Saturday that her parents weren't up at their cabin. The services started at 5:00 p.m. and her father rarely, if ever, went along. After church, her mother always made a meal and I was rarely invited for it. However, Bonnie was expected to be there and she typically helped finish the dishes. They lived a very secluded life and preferred to keep things that way.

This class was intended to determine whether the couples involved were actually ready to be married by the end of their scheduled sessions. Father O'Rourke was definitely able to uncover some troublesome issues. Bonnie would try to convince him that things would improve once she became removed from the environment she was living in. Our pending marriage, of course, was always the solution to the identified issues he would address. In hindsight, I'm surprised he didn't recommend that we pull the plug. He knew we were planning to have a large wedding and had already taken numerous steps along the way. He wondered why Bonnie hadn't spent more time at our intended residence, but she tried to convince him that she wasn't comfortable being defiant to her parents. We were given the okay to proceed with our wedding; but he likely did so with a high degree of reluctance.

Shortly before our wedding was to take place, Bonnie told me that she did not want my mother to be at the actual rehearsal which was to be held in the church the Friday night before. She didn't want to have a rehearsal dinner either. What seemed especially odd was that her parents seemed to like and respect my Mom; my mother was pretty hurt by this. However, being the supportive mother, she did not want to cause any type of disruption to her son's wedding.

It was the night before our wedding, on Friday the 13th, 1981. All of our planned attendants were gathered in the front entryway of the church waiting for the rehearsal to begin. It was scheduled to start at 6:00. However, Bonnie and her parents had not yet arrived. We were all getting a bit antsy. It became close to 7:00 and Bonnie, her two parents and her cousin, Laura, from Wisconsin Rapids came walking in. They were nearly an hour late. Father O'Rourke then hurriedly said, "Best Man"…and my brother Doug starts to move into place, "next, Matron of Honor" and Shirley starts to slowly move into place. As she does, Bonnie spoke up and said "No, Laura is my Maid of Honor." This caught me, and others, totally off guard.

I quickly moved in front of everyone and hurriedly made a moving gesture with my arms that was reminiscent of when a football kicker's given the "no good" sign for missing a field goal attempt. I then defiantly stated, "this is enough, the wedding is off." Doug was extremely upset and the others there were visibly stunned. I called the wedding off right there in the church entryway. Bonnie then said, "let's just leave it the way it was"…TOO LATE!! We then headed to a back room to meet privately with Father O'Rourke. He only reinforced my position. He clearly stated that he could no longer marry us. She pleaded to return things to the way they were anticipated, but there was no going back. You can hurt me and I'll likely come back, but when someone hurts someone very close to me, that's a different story. Here, my sister-in-law was overcoming her serious medical problems and was so proud to be filling the prestigious Matron of Honor role in our wedding. Bonnie had already hurt my Mom too. It turns out she had recently discussed the possibility of changing over to her cousin Laura with Sue from work. This is why Sue was considering backing out as one of her bridesmaids. She hadn't given me the specific reason when she'd called me earlier.

After coming back out, we gave the others the confirmation that our wedding would not be taking place. I headed to my mother's home to let her know. She was totally devastated and just couldn't believe what had happened. Being the great mother that she was, she did not want to see her son's expected wedding day be hampered in any way. Her first reaction was to have me give Bonnie a call and get the wedding back on. We told her that we had much yet to do that evening and Doug and Shirley promptly drove me back to my home in Oshkosh.

We expected Bonnie and her parents to show up at the house because there were a couple of pre-wedding presents that were being kept there. They didn't disappoint. Not long after we got inside they definitely made their presence felt for a short while. I just sat on a couch while her Dad was leaving with a microwave that we'd received; there was a brief confrontation. Doug said, "what kind of people are you?" and her Dad mumbled, "we're hard working people." They left shortly thereafter.

I was on the telephone most of the night calling people to tell them that I had cancelled the wedding. We each had planned to go in to work on the Monday after it. I was thankfully able to reach my boss and asked him to spread the word there before I came in. We agreed that I'd come in on Tuesday, rather than Monday. Here's another interesting point. Voice mail was not in vogue back then, so I needed to actually reach the people on the telephone to let them know what had happened. The only way I could leave a message was if someone answered the respective phone calls.

My good friend since junior high, Gary West, was going to be in Boston for work during the time of our wedding. He wanted to surprise me, but he's the one who ended up getting the biggest surprise. Upon heading to the Labor Temple, where our reception was to held, he reads a sign placed there which said: Jensen-Beyer wedding has been cancelled…he thought WHAT? I never attempted to call him because I wasn't expecting him to be able to attend. Gary's always had a very good sense of humor and he needed one in this instance. He and numerous other friends got with me for a special Saturday night of support. This was so very much appreciated. I felt bad for what I'd put the others involved with (what became a travesty) through. I used to tell people that I was divorced, but never married. It sure felt that way for quite some time.

I'll never forget the comment that the parent company's Corporate Controller told me over the telephone. He said, "I will always respect you for what you did…most people would have just went ahead with the wedding because of all of the associated complications involved." I recognize that it was the grace of God that saved me from making what would have been a serious mistake. Ironically, this took place on FRIDAY the 13th; a day normally besieged by superstitious thoughts. It ended up being a lucky day for me and it was still FOLLOWED BY VALENTINE'S DAY in 1981 (which was typically viewed as the most romantic day of the year). Bonnie, Sue, Father O'Rourke, her father, my brother Doug and my mother have since passed away. Bless each of their souls.

The house on Cedar Street.

You Must Answer This

∽ 10 ∾
JOSH GROBAN
and "AMAZING GRACE"

The first time that I heard Josh Groban sing was during half time of an NBA All-Star game. Here's this young man, with a once in a lifetime voice, just grabbing my attention. Years later, in the fall of 2004, we saw that he was coming to Milwaukee for a concert in late February of 2005. The date of the concert was February 27th. By this time, my wife Julie and I had become huge fans of his and Julie had bought all of his CDs. We were excited about the opportunity to see him perform live, even though it was during our unreliable winter weather season. More importantly, we were bothered by this specific concert date because we would normally be spending this evening with my mother Grace. February 27th was her birth date and she was to be turning 93. We made the decision to purchase tickets for this concert well in advance. Mom was living in a dementia/Alzheimers facility and knowing my mother very well...she would have wanted us to go. Little did we know that Mom would pass away on February 11, 2005.

It turns out that February 27th is also Josh Groban's birth date. He announced this during the performance. One of the songs he surprisingly sang that evening was Amazing Grace. This literally blew me away and the tears began to quietly flow down my face.

My wonderful Mother and Dad had three children. They were married in early January of 1929. This was the year of The Great Depression. My brother Doug was born in mid-January of 1930. In the summer of 1932, a daughter was born. My mother named her Charmaine; after the beautiful song from that era. Charmaine was only to live about two and a half months. She died of complications from pneumonia and I was told that my mother took this especially hard and that it tore her up for quite some time. Mom used to say that "she was just too smart for this world." With today's modern antibiotics, they likely could have saved her life. Ironically, my brother's wife of over 50 years, Shirley, is very close in age to Charmaine. Their birthdays are less than one month apart.

In the late 1940s and early 1950s, my Dad and brother were in the midst of tackling a huge project. My Mom and Dad had bought some property on the west side of town and made the decision to build a home there. Doug drew all of the blueprints and it was designed by my father. They were to work evenings, weekends and holidays. The style of the home was to be very unique and unconventional for its time. It was to feature a lot of interior and exterior stone work. Neither had ever previously even attempted to do any of this type of work. There was to be a good-sized sunken living room with numerous, large thermopane windows throughout its structure. The entire layout reflected a very open concept and it was to have a flat top roof. The home was based on a California ranch style design. They couldn't work in the winter until the house was enclosed. The only professional, paid-for work was the plastering. They dug the foundation by hand, did all of the wiring, installed all of the plumbing and heating, completed all of the masonry and hand-cut the pieces of stone that were used.

My Dad was a craftsman in the foundry industry. In an effort to top off the extensive floor to ceiling stone fireplace area of the home, he took on a task (referred to as the lost art of "drafting") to create an attention getting, iron-based statue to be featured at the far right corner of the actual fire pit. Both my father and multi-talented brother were working full-time at their respective jobs at the Neenah Foundry during the five plus year timeframe it took to complete the building of this home. My brother created impressive knotty pine ceiling beams with the use of chains and they incorporated acoustical tile and indirect lighting. They were, thankfully, able to enlist the help of some friends and family members and most commonly, my mother's considerable support...like pushing wheelbarrows.

During a doctor's visit in the fall of 1952 my mother was told that she was pregnant. When told of this news she said to the doctor, "I can't be pregnant!" He then supposedly said to her, "don't look at me...I had absolutely nothing to do with it." Needless to say, my Dad was very surprised, but I'm told he was also very proud. Here, my mother was 40 and my Dad was 46 and they were being kidded that were going to be having their own grandchild.

My Dad and brother were working on framing in a bathroom window on the eastside of the house when my mother went into labor. My Dad fainted and it was my brother that needed to take my mother to the hospital. Doug was also pretty proud of his little baby brother. Doug and Shirley were never able to have children of their own so, I guess I was brought into the world at that time for a number of different reasons.

My Dad and brother Doug at work building my parents home.

My Mother was a very special lady. Most of the people who got to know her over the years would say she fit the criteria of an "Amazing Grace." She always dressed classily and was commonly seen wearing a nice dress and high heels. She was a relentless worker who regularly cut her own large lawn with a push mower and was still shoveling her own snow well into her 80s; and this was usually very early in the morning. It was extremely difficult for her in losing my Dad. They were very close and I remember being brought up in a pretty stable environment. My Dad had his health issues, but neither of them were complainers. Rather, they were commonly reaching out to help others in need and at different times even had various family members living with them/us in their home.

Mom found various ways to help her pass the time after my Dad was gone. She and I became very close. She sure helped and cared for me a ton over the years. Living next door to my brother and sister-in-law enabled her to have some regular company, but her loneliness became more and more evident as time went on. I was married and living out of town and Doug and Shirley had their own busy lives spending

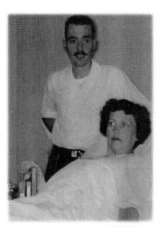

Doug and Mom in the hospital after my birth.

Mom after falling off curb into street.

important quality time at their beautiful cottage in North Central Wisconsin. She loved to go shopping and would visit with others in a mall, clothing store or jewelry shop. It wasn't unusual to see her taking a walk to the grocery store for some items. In fact, one time she walked all the way over to a Red Owl grocery store on the Southeast side of town (this had to be five miles one way). She always listened to the radio (religiously station WNAM) and loved watching the Lawrence Welk Show. She regularly drove her car up until November of 1996. A major turning point occurred when she fell and broke her right hip attempting to climb the front two steps of Doug and Shirley's home. She required emergency surgery on November 11th and never drove again after that. After this surgery, she lived with them for about eight weeks before moving back into her own home. During her recovery, she kept in pretty good spirits, but a couple of weeks before Easter of 1997 she told me on the phone that she had been noticing some trouble walking. We'd invited her, Doug and Shirley over for Easter Sunday. I clearly remember watching Mom limping very noticeably as she was walking up the front sidewalk to come into our home. I could not believe what I was seeing. On Monday morning, we promptly called the doctor and he said that we should bring her in right away. She required next day, emergency surgery on her other hip. It had basically deteriorated from excessive wear and tear and the over reliance on it during her recovery from prior surgery. My mother was never one to baby herself and a few months later, she fell head first onto the aggregate concrete street surface when she was bending over near the curb to pick up something that was in her lawn. For some time afterwards, she looked like she'd been badly beaten up in a fight.

The time had clearly come to urgently find another living environment for our Mom. We felt it would be best for her to move closer to Julie and myself here in Oshkosh. After inquiring about and visiting numerous options, we chose a nice, two bedroom apartment for her that was very near our home. This was fine for a short while, but Mom had reached a stage where she required more assistance. In the meantime, I was able to enlist some major help from a co-worker to get her house ready to be listed for sale. It sold by the spring of 1999. Mom was accepted into a very appealing looking assisted living facility nearby; only to be rejected from going back to it less than three months later after she experienced a couple of falls. I was thankfully able to get her into a wonderful dementia/Alzheimers facility (which had impressed me much earlier). This is where she spent the last four years of her life.

I regularly find myself quoting many of her numerous sayings and phrases to this day. When asked how she was doing she'd commonly answer, "I'm able to sit up and take nourishment." It was either this or she'd bluntly (but kiddingly say), "everybody I can." Two of my favorites are "you can choose your friends, but you can't choose your enemies" or "you can't make a silk purse out of a sow's ear."

I've been truly blessed to have been raised in such a caring family. My mother was given the responsibility of carrying a heavy torch for many years of my development as a person. She was always there to help and encourage me. I tried to thank her as best I could by steadfastly fighting to maintain her independence over the years and trying to be sure that she had the best quality of life possible during her declining years. I'm extremely proud to say that she was my mother and she will always be remembered by me and many others as one "AMAZING GRACE."

**Gary and Mom at Doug and Shirley's
50th wedding anniversary party.**

Mom on her 82nd birthday.

∂ 11 ∞
Autumn's In The Air…
IS THAT ROZO THE CLOWN?

We each have our favorite times of the year. For my taste, there's nothing like autumn. It usually seems to bring, what I like to refer to as, 'high energy weather' along with it. Julie and I got married on October 1st, and the freshness in the air during autumn is invigorating. Our wedding was going to be held outdoors and we aimed for a Saturday in October.

I've always been a huge fan of Halloween. It became kind of a bummer when I hit my teen years because I was supposedly outgrowing Halloween. It wasn't cool to be 'almost a grown up' and still be participating in this truly underappreciated holiday. I got it, but is Halloween just for kids? I heartily contest that no, it is not.

When I was a young child, my Godfather Jerry would walk with me around our neighborhood to help fill my bag with tasty treats. We lived at the far southwest end of a large outer court. There were over one hundred homes represented by its footprint. Then there was the inner court; with close to a hundred more. This was a paradise for a kid to take advantage of. I haven't even referenced the surrounding area that was filled with nice sidewalks and street lights.

The environment was safe and it was common to see van loads of kids being dropped off to penetrate this well-inhabited landscape. I loved dressing up in costume. My mother was pretty creative and I liked being "out there amidst" all of the excitement. A big deal for me was the anticipation of examining the contents of my annual haul. Butterfinger candy bars were number one on my list, with Heath bars coming in second. Baby Ruth bars were okay, too, but they came in well behind the yellow-wrapped, chocolate covered treasures. Getting a caramel apple that was secured with wax paper was always primo, but we learned to check for razor blades and this took away from the reckless spontaneity of biting into one of those tasty gifts from the Halloween Gods.

My Dad was suffering from some health issues as I was getting older. I wasn't into high school sponsored Halloween parties either. Things just got a bit more serious around home and I sure understood why. It was no biggy. I figured that my future enjoyment of this holiday was likely to come from both reflections of my past and watching other youngsters enjoy it. I was ready to move on.

When I went out to the bars in college, Halloween was clearly being celebrated with vigor and enthusiasm. Many of the costumes were pretty darn impressive. People were sure having fun with it. This got me very excited too. I loved dressing up in character. It became so much fun to "be and act" like another persona for a few hours. This got people out of their comfort zone in many cases. Of course, it wasn't they who did this or that, it was King Tut; or that was a lot of fun, but it was only because Luke Skywalker was the one involved.

Friends would have Halloween parties in their apartments or we'd meet up at different places to begin the night. It seemed to always be innocent fun, but it was considerable fun nonetheless. Some people shared no expense when it came to their costumes. I always looked forward to seeing the various output that was directly attributable to creative ideas. Many of these ideas turned into

elaborate ensembles or clever takeoffs from a theme.

My mother made a clown costume for me out of a white sheet that was freely sprinkled with large red spots. I incorporated some extensive red makeup, a large rubber nose and a flimsy, rimmed brown hat. The facial makeup was always critical and became the most enjoyable piece. This character became known as Rozo the Clown. I've had a ton of fun with him over the years. He even surfaced in our state's capitol city one year. Boy, do they know how to celebrate Halloween on State Street in Madison, Wisconsin! You just never know, when or, if Rozo will make a return visit at some point in the future. He's been known to, unexpectedly, just show up after disappearing for quite some time.

Rozo the Clown.

When I was engaged to Bonnie in late 1980, she and I both loved this time of year. Dressing up became a nice escape for us during the stress of our impending February wedding. After we broke up, I continued to enjoy the Halloween season and the changing colors of the leaves as we first moved into autumn. One late October day in 1985 I found this totally unexpected letter in my mailbox after I'd gotten home from work. It was from Bonnie. She initiated the contact with me and came across as her old self in this letter, saying all the right things and asking to meet with me at the Chalice Restaurant. As a friend had said to me, our relationship ended, but it had never truly finished. She was still living with her parents. I wasn't seeing anyone else at this time and was open to the idea. I told her that I would not drive into their driveway. We dated for awhile and even got re-engaged, but I was much less accepting this time around. It was still too much of the same old, same old and thankfully; our relationship was able to reach a final closure this time around. This was best for both of us.

Over the years, I've enjoyed playing many different characters. Three of my all-time favorites were: Pontius "Ponty" Pirate, the One-Eyed, Scar-faced Preacher and Big Mac McGwire. There were many times when I dressed in costume at work as well. This was usually pretty well received. I've never been afraid to poke some fun at myself. I've always tried to come across as approachable and I still believe that this is very important regardless of the circumstances which we may find ourselves in. I wasn't distant by nature, nor did I think of myself as being better than another person. Being in character seems to help take down people's barriers to communication.

We have this friend named Roy who consistently gets my vote for being the most innovative designer. How he regularly outdoes himself amazes me. One year he came up with a costume that he called Porta-Roy. He was a walking portable toilet. It covered the full ten yards for a quick first down. We're talking about the seat and its cover, the extended roll of toilet paper and of course, the flusher. He was completely dressed in white; so it was as sanitary as one could get.

We have a couple other friends who are known for holding incredible Halloween parties. Diane and Greg also happen to be outstanding cooks and the quality and quantity of the food they consistently provide caused me to inquire if they had an extra room where Julie and I could spend the

Bernard Brewer and the Fairy Princess.

night. This was because there had to be great leftovers for breakfast or lunch the next day.

Julie and I have continued the fun with being King Arthur and Guinevere, the 60s Rocker and his Girl, Arrrgh the Pirate and Missy, Julius Caesar and Calpurnia, The King and Queen of Hearts, Disco Danny Davelli and Dynamite Dolly Devine and Bernard "Bernie" Brewer and the Fairy Princess. We attempt to be ourselves the rest of the year. Compared to many of our wonderful holidays, Halloween is probably one of the most stress free, unless you count the stress that may be involved when you're determining what costume to wear. This shouldn't be stressful, though, if you give yourself enough time to make a selection.

What's wrong with having some unadulterated fun once in a while? Everyone needs to feature humor in their life; and the word 'feature' was not chosen by accident. I believe that there are too many times when we take ourselves too seriously. There are things in our life which are extremely serious and we have little choice but to deal with them accordingly. However, not everything warrants this type of treatment. Laughter is one of the best medicines that has ever existed and yet it's seldom prescribed. Let you be your own prescriber; don't just wait for others to make your day. There may even come a time, during autumn, when you look around and spot this crazy looking character. Don't be afraid to ask someone that may be near to you, excuse me, but IS THAT ROZO THE CLOWN?

❧ 12 ❧
YOU DID WHAT?

It was a nice summer evening in late July of 1987. We're fortunate here in Oshkosh to be one of the handful of cities which feature Lake Winnebago, the largest inland lake in Wisconsin. From late May through September an outdoor concert series takes place every Thursday night. This concept began in 1985 and it's always been set at a location in the city that was bordered by water, hence its name: Waterfest. The promoters have consistently been able to attract some excellent national bands to play here. I believe on this particular evening they'd gotten either Bachman Turner Overdrive or Foghat.

I went home to change clothes after work and headed over to the nearby concert grounds at around 5:30. They usually featured two to three bands for each of the evenings. The music started by six and concluded around ten. Not long after I'd arrived, I saw my cousin Bob. He's only a year younger than me and we'd always hit it off. I used to refer to him as kind of a second brother. He was there with a date. She seemed very nice and he said they'd met after she responded to a personals ad he'd placed in the local newspaper.

My cousin Bob placed a personals ad? First of all, he was very much of an introvert. Second of all, personals ads were quite uncommon at this time, at least around this area. Of all the people I knew, he would have been one of the last I'd guess to ever write such an ad. I must admit; I was impressed. A seed became planted in my mind through no conscious efforts of my own.

After calling off my scheduled wedding in February of 1981, I dated some different women. I've always met people pretty easily, but was also more on the cautious side when it came to getting too close to people. I'm definitely an extrovert by nature, but was more on the shy side when it came to approaching potential dating partners. I also hadn't experienced the necessary feelings to cause me to even attempt to bring any of those prior or subsequent relationships to a more serious level.

When my former fiancee, Bonnie, sent me an unexpected letter in late October of 1985 to get back together "to just talk", I was open to doing so. This was because I hadn't met anyone, since our break up, to fill the distracting void which was in my life. I knew it was there and was commonly bothered by it. It wasn't the fact that I was 34. It was the fact that I sincerely wanted to share my life with someone special.

I always tried to do the right things to put myself in the best possible position to enjoy a fulfilling life. College was a great experience and I viewed it as a means to an end. At that time, I was focused on getting through my undergraduate years in the least possible time with decent grades. Having a meaningful relationship during these years was not something I was interested in. Sure, I appreciated being around fun and attractive women in the bars, but to pursue anything serious in this regard wasn't at all where I was at.

After graduating and being offered a responsible, career-type job, I became more inclined to find a nice woman to potentially develop an ongoing relationship with. I've always been picky, but I believed that I'd be a pretty good catch too. My value system and level of integrity has always meant a great deal to me when it came right down to it. I hadn't moved up to Green Bay for the first seven months and it kept my life a bit more scattered. I was dating a girl who lived in my home town and I didn't see it going anywhere. We broke up shortly after I moved. I enjoyed going out there on Wednesdays, but would still come back most weekends and go out with friends around the Fox River Valley.

I had gotten more than frustrated with the bar scene. Here I was, a very responsible person with respectable goals, but it usually didn't seem to matter there. Everyone was equal in this environment until there was some type of break through where such consideration was given its due. I'd finally come to realize that it is what it is. It had reached a point where I was trying to make it more than what it's intended to be. Bars can provide a meeting place for friends and a spot to have some fun. I'd thoroughly enjoyed them over the years. However, anything more meaningful to derive from these types of settings is typically incidental and commonly quite uncontrollable.

I believe I was meant to talk with my cousin Bob that Thursday evening at Waterfest. It was this unforgettable Godincidence which became the catalyst for me to pursue a previously unrecognized alternative for meeting well-matched and like-minded women. I decided to write a very straightforward and

Cousin Bob (left) and Gary.

highly specific ad in our local newspaper. I was still looking to find one special woman to hopefully share my life with. Thanks to Bob, this became viewed by me as a legitimate option which I'd never thought of pursuing. Not that many people were told that I'd written this ad in July of 1987. I wasn't the least bit embarrassed about writing it, but I didn't think it was other people's business either. The ad was to run for a total of 10 days and it cost me $78.10.

The responses were to be sent to a blind post office box number. Shortly after this ad was printed a female co-worker, named Katie, came into my office, shut the door behind her and forcefully said to me, "was that you?" I said, "was that me what?" She said, "was that you who wrote that personals ad in the Northwestern?" After admitting to her that it likely was me who wrote the ad she was referring to, she told me that it sounded just like me and I thought to myself...I guess I must have done a pretty good job of writing it then.

17 Personals

HI! I'm a 34 year old, single male, never married, 6', 175 lbs. who's honestly looking to meet a sincere, attractive, fun-loving, mature-thinking woman, 24-34, to share life with. Interests include music (especially rock-n-roll), dancing, dining, and such sports as, tennis, golf, and biking. I'm a respected professional with high standards, who enjoys life and appreciates simple things. Non-smokers preferred and individuals with dependents need not reply. Please send replies to Box Q-2, c/o The Oshkosh Northwestern.

Gary's personals ad.

After about a week or so later, I'd received absolutely no responses to my ad. I was quite bummed. When I called to inquire, they sheepishly apologized for a mistake that was made on their end. They promptly, albeit belatedly, mailed me seven responses to the ad. I had promised myself that I would respectfully attempt to answer any of the responses I received. They were nice enough to take the time to write and send their response, let alone accept the risk of doing so. I would at least offer to meet with each of the them and potentially take them out for a nice meal.

I read over each of the responses. A few of them got me excited. There was one in particular which really captured my attention. Her name was Julie and she included a picture, as most of the others had. I liked what she had to say. She was a college graduate and an established English teacher. Julie said that she was in the last stage of becoming divorced and that it would be final very shortly. This did not turn me off and was not one of the criteria I'd identified as being important to me in my ad. With the inadvertent passage of time, however, I was concerned that she may already believe that I'd been turned off by this. I tried to call her a number of times and wasn't even able to leave a message. I was very frustrated by this and thought, thanks a lot <u>Oshkosh Northwestern</u>…your screw up possibly caused me to miss the opportunity to meet a special lady.

I used to coach girl's softball and there were a number of attractive women on the respective teams. Asking any of them for a date was just something I didn't pursue. Some of them had become friends, but were nothing more than that. The first woman I got a hold of had written that she enjoyed playing softball and that her friends thought she was pretty good. Her name was Geri, and her humility impressed me. She ended up being the president of a local singles club. She'd had her stomach stapled because of weight issues and had an extremely restrictive diet. Nothing against Taco Bell, but this is where she wanted to go out to eat. She had a small burrito and a diet RC cola. When I dropped her off she said something like, I probably won't see you again, right? I told her that I had just begun the process and intended to honor each of the responses I'd received. There definitely wasn't a match here though.

The second woman I was able to make contact with was named Sandy. I took her to Otto Grunski's Annual Polish Festival in nearby

Menasha. She was a nice person and we enjoyed our date. I dropped her off on good terms, but made no other type of commitment to her. She understood the circumstances.

It was after this time that I finally was able to reach Julie. I called her on Tuesday evening, August 11th and we talked for two and one half hours. I explained what had happened and apologized for the delay in reaching her. Being a teacher, she was off for the summer. She had been spending periods of time at her parents' home. They were providing her with some welcome support and consideration as her impending divorce was nearing its conclusion. Our first date was on Friday, August 14th. It was spectacular.

One evening, not too long thereafter, Julie and I were visiting in the basement of my house when the doorbell rang. It was Sandy and she wanted to show me her new car. Julie and I came to the top of the stairs together; the landing was by the front door. I wasn't expecting her and was surprised to see her standing there. This was awkward and I introduced them to each other. I called Sandy the next day and explained that Julie and I had really connected. I told her that she was a very nice person and wished her well, but also told her that I would not be dating any other women but Julie at this point.

I attempted to contact each of the other respondents and told those that I was able to reach the same thing. My intention was not to create a dating pool. A great deal of thought and consternation was put into the writing of this ad. It was submitted for a much more specific purpose. My answer to the associated question of YOU DID WHAT?, is simply this. There never were any safeguards involved with the unconventional effort I made to meet "that special woman" to possibly share my life with. In fact, the odds of its success were likely very low. I contend that Julie and I were clearly meant to meet; but there's another major lesson that needs to be learned here. We each needed to step outside of our comfort zone and do something that was quite atypical in order for us to do so.

You Must Answer This

᜶ 13 ᜷
What Do You Mean
YOU CAN'T REACH HER??

You've heard the phrase 'timing is everything.' Have you ever felt you were just so close to getting something important accomplished, but for whatever reason you couldn't get it done. Depending on the degree of importance involved; the frustration level can be considerable. There are many times when the associated success or failure is independent of your control.

I'm very proud of a number of things in my life. My wonderful parents, my brother Doug and sister-in-law Shirley, some prior work accomplishments and importantly, what I stand for as a person. We're only one little pebble on the beach of life, but it's clearly up to us to make something happen from the opportunities that are available to us. I'm most proud of doing whatever was needed from me in order for my wife Julie and I to initially meet back in August of 1987.

I've always tried to be a decent person. Respecting the lives of others is primary to our existence. Living within our respective environments presents our primary challenge; it's going after life that's directly dependent on us. Taking things for granted is a common trait. We all have basic wants and needs. Maslow's defined hierarchy does a great job of explaining the fundamental prioritization involved. Regardless, most things will require some degree of effort on our behalf to get accomplished.

I've been fortunate to have realized the energy generated from self-actualization in a number of different ways. I did well in school and made the Dean's Llist a number of times in college. The rewards were pretty simplistic, but they sure felt good. They were based on the recognition of a specifically defined achievement. Getting promotions at work not only meant better pay, they represented a formal recognition of accomplishment. It wasn't the title, as such, but it was the comparative stature being recognized in the environment that became important.

The concept of entitlement is foreign to me. We all take things for granted, but to expect that most things will take care of themselves is ludicrous. Typically, it is our efforts which can lead to good fortune, not that we always simply deserve good fortune. Our reality in this country is based on life, liberty and the pursuit of happiness. The key word here is 'pursuit.' We usually need to pursue something. We pursue an education, we pursue a relationship, we pursue a job, we pursue finding a better or different place to live.

My life had been going along pretty well. I was blessed with good friends. I'd reached a number of my goals and believed I was on the right track career-wise. There was clearly one thing that was missing, however. It wasn't leaving a very small hole either. The associated frustration level was considerable. Meeting a special woman to share my life with had definitely become my biggest challenge. There is no cookbook to get this done, no specific directions to follow and worst of all, there are no guarantees of success.

Does this mean I needed to give up trying to find that elusive person? I wasn't looking for a buried treasure, but it sure felt like it. I had a responsible job and was a reliable individual. Did something else need to be given up in my life in order for this to potentially happen? There weren't any hints that I was finding, let alone receiving an answer to my prayers. After talking with my cousin Bob that fateful Thursday evening at Waterfest in the summer of 1987, I was given the necessary seed which then required germination. It is this germination which caused me to pursue what became the heartfelt writing and prompt submission of a personals ad. I thankfully exhibited a 'sense of urgency' in this matter.

The process of forwarding me the associated responses to this ad got unnecessarily complicated by an internal glitch within the Oshkosh Northwestern offices. I'd received no responses for the first week to ten days. I contacted them and they looked into it and found that there was a failure somewhere in their procedures. They apologized up and down and sent me out the responses that they'd received.

As for where Julie fits into this scenario, she first read my ad one evening after sitting down to relax on a sofa in her apartment. Julie is one who reads the newspaper, as well as other things, very carefully. To this day, she doesn't miss very much. She later told me that she had been regularly praying to God, asking for his help in meeting someone compatible to share her life with. This was at a time when personals ads around this area were unheard of, especially within the confines of our very traditional local newspaper.

Julie has told me this story many times. After she read my ad she said she heard a very calm, but commanding, androgynous sounding voice which clearly said, "YOU MUST ANSWER THIS." She swears to this day that she's not heard this voice either before or since that one very specific time.

I was particularly impressed after both reading Julie's response to my ad and seeing her nice picture. She was very attractive and definitely came across as the type of person I was looking for. Julie said in her letter that she'd been previously married. This definitely didn't bother me. At the time she responded, she was well into the process of completing a very difficult and trying divorce. It was to become final near the end of August, and I appreciated her making the effort to at least talk with me under the circumstances. I was thirty four myself at the time and had already come very close to being divorced in 1981. I was more than convinced that if I would have went through with my intended marriage, there likely would have been a divorce not too far down the road; if not even an annulment. Regardless, I thought GREAT…she probably thinks I haven't called her because of this reason. I was very concerned that she thought I was already turned off.

I had tried, unsuccessfully, a few different times to reach her. Because it was summertime, she had been spending some time at her parents' home in North Fond du Lac. This was certainly understandable, but I had no knowledge of this. Finally, on Tuesday night, August 11, 1987, I was able to reach her on the telephone. As I recall it was about 6:30. We talked for two and one half hours…THAT IS RIGHT…we clearly hit it off and the conversation flowed very comfortably. I told her what had happened, with the delay I had experienced in receiving responses from the newspaper. We laugh about it now, but we almost got caught up in some timing related complications ourselves.

Our first date was Friday night, August 14th. I picked Julie up at her apartment on the northeast side of Oshkosh. We went to an outstanding

July 28, 1987

Hello! (I was going to begin with "Dear Sir", but that sounds so formal.)

First of all, let me state that I do feel a bit uncomfortable writing this note. I have never responded to an ad like this before. Allow me to begin by telling you something about myself. I am a 30-year old high school English teacher. (Don't be turned off by that stereotype — I am fun-loving and attractive.) I am currently going through a divorce that will be final in August. However, I do not have any children.

As you stated in the ad, you are looking for "a sincere, attractive, fun-loving, mature-thinking woman." This may sound conceited, but I do possess many of those qualities. I love to go out to dinner, dances (especially '50's-'60's music), movies and plays. I thoroughly enjoy socializing, but I like my share of quiet times too.

Physically, I am fairly attractive. I am 5'5" tall, 110 lbs., golden blond hair and green eyes. (I am enclosing a year book photo ('86-'87) so you can see my appearance.)

(over)

The response to my ad.

70

Oriental restaurant just outside of town. This restaurant has since burned down and been replaced by a car wash. After enjoying a nice meal and some great conversation we headed over to a cocktail lounge that was in the lower level of the Pioneer Hotel and Resort. There was a good band playing there that evening and we danced a lot. To say that we hit it off would be major understatement. I was very attracted to both her personality and her appearance. She was clearly a very classy lady and I

Julie's picture with her response.

was most proud to be with her. We seemed to thoroughly enjoy each other's company and it seemed like we knew each other much longer than we had.

We are always accountable, but timing is everything when it comes to the successful meshing of our efforts and external circumstances. Still, our pursuit of something involves us actively doing things to help make that something happen. It may be just a one-time effort or a series of efforts over a period of time. We definitely need to do our part; sometimes it may even be unconscionably, but it this which at least helps to potentially facilitate it. We may need to be at a certain place during a certain time or chose to do something different than we'd intended to do. Thereafter, if and when something is meant to happen…it will happen. Thankfully, Julie and I were meant to meet and she and I took some steps to facilitate it.

Our first date would successfully compete with anyone's. We've been happily and thankfully together ever since. Julie and I proudly celebrated our twenty fifth wedding anniversary on October 1, 2013. I humbly offer this free tip for each of you. If you're trying to get in touch with someone and you've become frustrated because YOU CAN'T REACH HIM or HER. My advice to you is…be sure to keep trying!!

You Must Answer This

৬৩ 14 ৩০
The 2:30 PHONE CALL On a FRIDAY AFTERNOON IN JANUARY Of 2008

My mother spent the last four years of her life in a dementia/Alzheimers facility here in Oshkosh. When Julie and I would visit, I noticed that it was becoming harder for me to simply get up from a chair. I thought it was because I was just getting older, but I was only in my early 50s. This had become more noticeable in other circumstances as well, because getting up was much easier if I could push off from something like the arms of a chair. In early December of 2007, we had our first significant snowfall of the season. I used our blower and about six hours later, I detected some unusual chest discomfort. This was on a Saturday and the discomfort was still there on Monday morning. I called to get an appointment with our doctor. I was able to get in to see one of his assistants that same afternoon. She checked me over and everything seemed okay. Near the end of this appointment, I first mentioned the issue I'd been experiencing when trying to stand up. She didn't take this lightly and recommended both a spinal MRI and setting up an appointment with a neurologist. The MRI came back fine, but the neurologist gave me an electromyogram (EMG) to check for other issues. It was determined that I had some type of myositis (or muscle disease). My symptoms were such that he strongly suggested I schedule a biopsy of my right quadriceps muscle. Julie and I discussed this and a biopsy was done in early January. We did some internet research on myositis because we were both unfamiliar with it. Some types were more disturbing than others and we prayed for the best.

On Friday afternoon, January 18th, I was thinking about the upcoming weekend. At about 2:30 the telephone rang and on the other end was a Dr. Barend Lotz from the University of Wisconsin Medical Center in Madison. He introduced himself as a neuro-muscular specialist and said he was calling regarding the results from my thigh muscle biopsy. The results confirmed our worst fear of Inclusion Body Myositis (aka IBM).

As long as I can remember, my mother had been such an independent person. It was extremely difficult watching her change into someone who became so dependent on the help of others. The change was gradual, but steady. Things had been very stressful on two major fronts for some time. I was no longer in the corporate world, but the collateral damage from it had left its ineradicable marks. In the fall of 2001, I was diagnosed with Graves Disease (a version of hyperthyroidism; an overactive thyroid condition). During the same timeframe, I was focused on proactively helping my mother make the best out of some deteriorating circumstances. We were always very close and the fallout from pervasive stress was taking its toll.

The company where I worked was bought out by investment bankers near the end of the second quarter of 2001. This brought about some major changes and increased the already significant day to day stress level there. By the end of 2002 they decided to actively put their investment up for sale and my position was eliminated exactly one week before Christmas. Merry Christmas wasn't even said. My wife and I were actually relieved because she saw firsthand what the combination of these two stress components was doing to me.

By the grace of God, I was introduced to a major change of pace home-based business opportunity in April of 2003. By May 1st we had created an S Corporation. It was intriguing, exciting, and reasonably challenging. Most importantly, it was fun while bringing in some nice additional income for us. We got involved in some different aspects of the business including; business building, face-to-face product retailing and participation in some trade and home and garden shows.

The caregivers at the facility my mother was at were awesome to her. I couldn't have asked for more in this regard. It was obvious near the end of 2004 that her condition had reached a point of no return. It was getting harder and harder for us to see her worsen. Then a new variable came into the mix. My only brother was formally diagnosed with cirrhosis of the liver around this same time. My mother was re-classified for hospice care at the facility in early February. She died in the early afternoon of Friday, February 11, 2005.

My brother Doug was in pretty bad shape at that time and he was barely able to attend Mom's funeral. He and my awesome sister-in-law Shirley suffered through his deteriorating health issues, but he was able to make it another eighteen months and died on September 22, 2006. This amount of additional time seemed implausible for him in February of 2005. Initially, he couldn't understand why I had consciously moved beyond attempting to get a job back in the corporate accounting world. He certainly meant well believing I was wasting my talents and turning my back on my advanced education and experience. In a reasonable time, he saw his brother much happier being away from the wear and tear of the corporate grind. He'd been there himself for many years.

For the first hour after receiving the call from Dr. Lotz, I was pretty devastated. My wife was still at work and I wanted to tell her this news, face to face, when she got home. I called my sister-in-law and she was wonderful. She told me to stay positive and things would work out. I then called two other close friends for their badly needed support. The first was former co-worker Bob Snyder. He was always full of wisdom and seemed to know the right things to say. Next, I called respected confidant and associated business owner Keith Revak from Belle Vernon, Pennsylvania. Like Shirley and Bob, Keith is a man of unwavering faith. He proceeded to give me more encouragement. I told each of them that my immediate goal was to get my head in a better place by Monday morning.

I then called a holistic naturopath in town to set up an appointment. I had previously been recommended to her by a couple we helped bring into our business from Ripon, Wisconsin. My brother and sister-in-law had also been to see her and were very impressed. When I called, I was told that I needed to have what is called a CEDSA (computerized electro dermal stress analysis) test done. Their first opening for this was in June and I took the appointment. Just twenty minutes later, they called back because they'd gotten a cancellation for February 11th (which was less than a month away). I was extremely excited about this opportunity and quickly claimed the appointment. I took this as a major positive sign from God. What also did not go unnoticed by me at that time was that February 11th was also my mother's dying day in 2005.

When Julie got home, I told her of the call. At first she was stunned, but she got herself composed very quickly. She then strongly said, "we will beat this." I wasn't able to get my head in as good of a place as I wanted to by

Monday, but it was in decent shape by Tuesday morning. Throughout the weekend we focused on positive things and watched some old Seinfeld reruns. We watched the movie Breakfast at Tiffany's on Saturday evening. Julie had recently purchased the video and I had never seen it before. I distinctly remember us recalling and talking about a Seinfeld episode where character George Costanza weaseled his way into a family's apartment and took an uninvited seat on a couch in their living room as they were watching this rented movie. George was in a book club and was pre-occupied with taking this urgent shortcut because he hadn't actually read the book. Each night, two reruns of Seinfeld episodes were shown beginning at 10:00. I don't know how many Seinfeld episodes were made over the years, but there were many of them. The first rerun shown on that Sunday night was the one which involved George and Breakfast at Tiffany's. This is the honest truth. I will never forget it. We took it as another sign that things were going to be okay. By the end of the weekend, I'd attempted to contact friends and relatives to tell them of my diagnosis.

Meeting holistic naturopath Nicki Jansma on February 11, 2008, has been one of the greatest blessings of my life. She is such an intelligent, positive and well-informed individual. Like my wife, she's consistently reinforced and encouraged my inner strength and positive beliefs. There is absolutely no doubt in my mind that her specific input and recommended natural supplementation has helped me immeasurably. I've been seeing Nicki at her Remedies facility every 8 to 12 weeks for regular follow up. Since this time, I have come to have a great deal of respect for her as a treasured friend, as well as a health advisor. My strong endorsement of Nicki's services is supported by the fact that there currently is a 14- to 15-month new patient waiting list to get in to see her. She focuses on helping people who are dealing with more difficult health-related issues. Her reputation has brought in patients from across the Midwest. Nicki's sincere passion and God blessed talents for helping others is incredible.

Julie and I first met with Dr. Lotz in Madison, Wisconsin, in late March of 2008. He and his assistant were both very blunt and clinical. I was told in no uncertain terms that this disease was both progressive and degenerative. He said that there was no known cause, cure or effective treatment identified to that point.

He discussed the fact that many people with this disease experience what's called dysphasia or an inability to swallow as the condition progresses. We had just returned from spending Easter vacation in Arizona the day before this doctor appointment. The night before returning home, Julie called her mother and was told that our little dog, Chelsea, whom they'd been watching for us, had passed and that her body had been taken to their vet. We picked up her frozen remains and took them to our vet's office to be cremated prior to heading for Madison. The tone of this visit was not one of hope, but rather one of resignation. We walked out of the clinic with our tails between our legs. Shortly after we got back in the car and headed for home, Julie defiantly said to me again, "we're going to beat this." This was a very tough period for us.

There is still no medically identified cause, cure or treatment for this inflammatory muscle disease. That 2:30 CALL ON FRIDAY AFTERNOON IN JANUARY OF 2008 was most disturbing, but one should never forget that it is God who remains all powerful. Also, our support systems are invaluable to us. Genuine belief and a person's attitude will always help them get through the difficult things they'll be faced with in their lives. One should not lose their spirit when there is still reason for hope. There definitely is reason for hope.

Our wonderful little Chelsea.

You Must Answer This

⚕ 15 ⚖
50 YEARS In The Foundry Industry

It was mid-July of 1971. My Dad was to be recognized as the featured guest of honor at a special dinner at The Valley Inn in Neenah and presented with an award by The American Foundry Society (AFS) for dedicating 50 years of his life to the foundry industry. We weren't sure until right before the day of this scheduled event, if he'd even be able to attend. He was so noticeably ill at this point and was actually dying of advanced stage colon cancer in the hospital. He had just officially retired from working at the Neenah Foundry Company.

Because of the special nature of the circumstances, Dad was temporarily released from the hospital to be able to be deservedly honored by his peers. At the time he was one of only three people in the state of Wisconsin to have reached this achievement. Both my brother Doug (who worked 28 years at the same place as my Dad) and myself were very proud to be there. Dad's personalized plaque says, "Men Like You Make The World Go Round."

When I was a kid my father would always take the time to hit baseballs to me in the side yard of our home after work. During the summer, I was usually right there to greet him with a bat, ball and glove to be sure he didn't get started doing something else first. He spent most of his days working in a hot foundry environment and got pretty tired by the end of the day. After all, my Dad was 47 when I was born, and by the time I wanted him to hit me baseballs, he was approaching his mid-fifties. He would take me to Milwaukee Braves baseball games and even played my position in Little League during a fathers vs. sons game at the age of 57.

He was extremely well-liked and highly respected by the people who got to know him. He never had the opportunity to make it to high school and graduated through the eighth grade. Dad was the oldest of eight children and he admirably handled a great deal of responsibility as he was growing up. He wasn't the biggest guy in stature, but he would stand up to the biggest of obstacles when he believed he was right.

Dad worked in the Core Room and it was here that intricate molds were made for many of the parts and accessories used by heavy machinery and sophisticated equipment. He became a master craftsman in this regard and understood the strengths and weaknesses of different compilations of sand and chemicals. He became the "go to" guy when questions arose in the environment. Internal and external chemical engineer-types came to him for advice.

He ended up being named Core Room Superintendant over all three plants involved with the company's operation. There was a ton of stress involved and I remember him coming home sometimes and just needing to sit outside on his chase lounge for awhile. He was never one to avoid challenges, but he would face them head on regardless if this was personnel related or production related. The workforce involved a number of seasonal workers and the nature of the work resulted in a significant turnover of employees.

I remember being in the kitchen when my Dad and Mom first talked about his diagnosis of colon cancer. The prognosis was not very good, but my Dad was never a quitter and he wasn't about to change. He developed a hobby of making unique and eye-catching lamps. The original home that he and my brother built part-time over a five plus year period had a flat-top roof. Over time, there were some issues with leaking and my brother designed and drew-up the associated details for a beautiful addition which effectively brought a second floor with attic space to the home. It was pretty neat looking before, but this addition was so complementary that it clearly stood out impressively on its corner lot.

The addition was completed about a year before my Dad passed. His talents incorporated the use of a spiral stairway for internal access to the second floor. This stairway was built from foundry components, but there was a complication. The rise associated with the steps wasn't conducive to a smoothly flowing handrail. Dad designed a means for successfully overcoming this obstacle. Mom and Dad purchased the carpeting for the second floor, but it did not get installed until after he'd passed away.

After work and on weekends, he would regularly climb the stairway and spend time designing and fabricating some very attractive custom lamps and fixtures. He had entrepreneurship on his mind and purchased some lamp-associated components. He developed a slogan for his operation…"see Beyer and see better" and got some business cards to pass out. I also remember another slogan that he'd use. It was "Beyer lights the dark

B EYER

Lamp & Gifts

MANUFACTURER CONVERSATION LAMPS

103 S. PLUMMER CT.
NEENAH, WIS.

PHONE PA 27447

BEYER

Dad's business card.

places." He named his business Beyer Lamp and Gifts. He approached some businesses and placed some of the fruits of his labor of love out on consignment. In fact, he even worked out an arrangement with Reilly Furniture in Appleton regarding his attractive, small Franklin stove lamps. He placed promotional ads for these lamps in newspapers and trade magazines, where someone could either buy them already assembled or else ready to assemble.

Unfortunately, he never got the chance to pursue this much further. It reached a point where the pain from the cramps associated with his cancer became too difficult to overcome. He had gotten a colostomy associated with the surgery, but he didn't let this slow him down. This was just another obstacle that he stood up to. The latter obstacle became too pervasive. He was to spend periods in an out of the hospital. It didn't matter if he was visited by the President of the company, another co-worker, a temporary subordinate, a neighbor, a friend or acquaintance; he always treated them with respect and dignity.

I was to be beginning my first year of college in September of 1971 and was scheduled for a freshman orientation day complete with a couple of placement-type exams on Tuesday, August 3rd. My

My Dad with his plaque.

The home that my Dad and brother designed and built (along with its later 2nd floor addition that was designed by my brother).

Mother had asked a neighbor friend if he'd drive me there and back as he was also scheduled for business school orientation on that same day. Between exams we grabbed some lunch and when we returned were asked by a test proctor, "Are either of you Gary Beyer?...(then) you need to go home right away." As we were approaching my parent's home I noticed my mother and our pastor standing in the driveway. My father had passed away while I was gone.

His funeral service was held in Neenah and his burial service was 25 minutes away in Oshkosh. The procession of cars on the highway was extraordinary...I'll never forget it! I've said for many years, "If I could be half the man that my father was, I'd be successful." Dad was a man of integrity who never saw himself as better than anyone else. His spending 50 YEARS IN THE FOUNDRY INDUSTRY is just one of the things he's remembered for. What he stood for will always be my fondest memory. I will never forget him.

My Dad with his two boys at recognition dinner.

∂ 16 ∞
STEPPIN' UP In 1982

It was early Saturday morning, April 17, 1982. I was about to take my very first flight. This flight was to leave Chicago's O'Hare Airport at 7:00 a.m. My good friend Paul and I were going to be heading out to San Francisco after changing planes in Denver. Actor Fernando Lamas was on our flight from Chicago. Singer/songwriter Chuck Berry was announced on our flight to San Francisco. We arrived at our destination at about 10:30 Pacific standard time.

Little did I know it, but 1982 was truly to become one of the most memorable years of my life. The incredible week's vacation in San Francisco will never be forgotten. What followed later in this particular year will always stand out for me as well.

The timing of this trip couldn't have been any better. After calling off my wedding in early 1981 this extremely enjoyable vacation with Paul was just what I needed. It was truly exhilarating and much more than I ever could have expected. He was awesome to travel with. After picking up our rental car, we checked into our motel and got situated. Paul's an outstanding planner and was always open to doing different things; yet, he was so well-prepared that were weren't about to miss any 'must see' attractions during our limited time there.

To get oriented to the area, we started on a 49-mile tour of the city that first afternoon. Being on top of his game, Paul was already aware of the 15th annual Cherry Blossom Festival that was underway in Japantown. We spent considerable time there while treating ourselves to some great food (this was a constant theme during our trip). From there we covered a major portion of the tour route. For whatever reason, I was quite sick when we got back to the hotel, and we ended up just winding down a bit, watching a movie in the room.

The next day we got up early and went to the top of Twin Peaks and then covered the balance of the tour. What a town!! Around 11:30 we

Gary in a cable car.

headed for Candlestick Park, the home of the San Francisco Giants baseball team. We were fortunate on a number of accounts. First, it was Cap Day. Second, the weather was absolutely fantastic being in the high 60s to low 70s. There were 39,000 people there and we were able to see the great Tom Seaver pitch for the Cincinnati Reds against the Giants. Getting there early, we'd walked around the stadium and were able to have a brief conversation with former Brewers player, Jim Wohlford, who was loosening up in the outfield prior to the start of the game. The Giants ended up winning 4-2 and we saw Reggie Smith and Darrell Evans hit home runs for the home team.

After returning, we took an extensive walk around the area. We had a "memorable" East Indian meal at Tarik's. I normally love spicy food, but one of the sauces was over the top. We'd taken our first of many cable car rides back to Van Ness Street before eating. The next day we took cable cars to Chinatown. After returning to the motel, we walked down to Fisherman's Wharf and took a Red and White Cruise of the Bay area. Paul had been

One of the most spectacular views in San Francisco.

advised be sure and have a meal at Scoma's and their cioppino was outstanding. There were pictures of celebrities all over this place. We finished the evening by completing all of the possible cable car transit routes in San Francisco.

During the remainder of our trip, we visited Sausalito and traveled over the Golden

Gate Bridge. We spent time in Muir Woods National Park; this spot is a must see. Paul was adventuresome and not the least bit intimidated with driving the breathtaking Highway One along the coast. We went to Napa Valley and toured the Christian Brothers Winery and tasted five different wines there. This area was beautiful and distinctive in scenery, character and land structure. Heading south, we went to Vallejo, Berkeley and Oakland.

Neither of us will ever forget a comment that we heard one student making to another as we were walking on the University of California campus. "How disenchanting," was loudly stated in an exasperating-type manner. We stopped and looked at each other rather dumbfounded; it seemed appropriate at Berkeley.

We enjoyed our morning breakfasts; which we ate every day at some different local restaurant. The seventeen mile scenic tour of the Monterey Peninsula was seemingly too good to be true. It ended at the extravagant Pebble Beach Golf Course. The weather was consistently pleasant during our stay and the picture taking opportunities were exceptional. Considerable time was spent at the beautiful Golden Gate Park area and we drove down the renowned Lombard Street on a couple of different occasions. Paul and I left San Francisco on Saturday afternoon, April 24th, at 3:00 p.m. We were satisfied that we did it justice.

Being a long-time fan of major league baseball and especially of the Milwaukee Brewers, I will always fondly remember the year of 1982. Their team, known as Harvey's Wallbangers, played exciting baseball during this time. They ended up earning the right to play for the American League championship by winning the final game of the regular season, holding off a dramatic charge by the Baltimore Orioles. They played the California

Ticket stub for final game of the American League Championship playoff–Brewers vs. Angels.

Scoreboard after Brewers became American League Champs in 1982.

Angels in a best of five series to determine which team would go on to the heralded World Series.

The Brewers were returning home down two games to none on October 7th. They had to win each of the remaining games in Milwaukee to win their first (and only) American League title. Thankfully, I had the opportunity to get four tickets for each of these games. A combination of friends were offered the chance to purchase tickets and join me. One friend, Steve, was as big of a fan as I was and I'd offered him the opportunity to attend each of the games. In fact, we both stayed overnight at his sister's place in Milwaukee during this time. These critical playoff games were played on three consecutive days.

The Brewers won the first two games; to tie the series at two games apiece. This set the stage for a Sunday, mid-afternoon finale on October 10th. The Brewers were down 3-2 going into the home half of the seventh inning. The crowd was pretty restless. One of their star players, Cecil Cooper, delivered a clutch base hit which drove in the tying and go ahead runs. The team held on to win the game 4 to 3 and the place went absolutely bonkers when it was over. After Sunday's dramatic playoff win a huge celebration erupted. We drove around town for a bit, basking in the euphoria; car horns were honking, people were ecstatic and the suds were steadily flowing. We visited The Steppin Up Bar on Oklahoma Avenue and had a really good time there. What a fantastic day! It remains the unequivocal number-one-ranked highlight of my treasured sports memories.

The World Series matched the venerable St. Louis Cardinals against the Brewers. As with the playoff series, I was able to secure four tickets for each of the three potential games that would be played in Milwaukee. However, this was to be a best of seven series. The Cardinals were to have the home field advantage if the Series went to seven games. The Brewers went up three games to two in what became known as "The Suds Series." The excitement was building, but the team lost the final two games that were played in St. Louis. This is the only time that the Brewers have been in a World Series.

The extra special memories from this awesome year concluded with attending The Who concert in Milwaukee on Wednesday night, December 8th thanks to Gary Ludwig, my good friend since college. They were always one of my very favorite bands and to see them perform live was a real treat. Being a drummer for many years, I would have loved to see Keith Moon play in person. Unfortunately, he was dead at that time, but his replacement, Kenny Jones, was fabulous.

Words alone can never do justice to the numerous views (like the ones from Coit Tower), the dramatic hills and the overall charm involved with the city of San Francisco. We left there but a part of our hearts will always remain in that environment. The baseball season of 1982 was special. Being able to attend each of the six playoff and World Series games that were played in Milwaukee was icing on the cake. As it was best and probably most simply stated by the stage announcer after their performance at Woodstock in 1969, "ladies and gentlemen...The Who." By any stretch of my imagination, there was some major STEPPIN' UP done in 1982. It definitely stands out as one of the most unforgettable years of my life.

You Must Answer This

✂ 17 ✂
The ATTENTION GETTING LETTER Received On a Friday in October

All through our lives we learn important things. Some are recognized as more important than others. We learn how to eat with a knife, fork and spoon, when to use the bathroom, where to find some new clothes, what types of food we enjoy the most, why we need to put a jacket on and who your favorite high school teacher is. These all sound pretty simple. The key word here is 'sound' because, at certain times, many of these things won't 'seem' so simple.

My point is, when something just sounds good to us, we haven't yet been able to internalize it. When it reaches a stage where it seems good we are beginning to feel it for ourselves. It's important for each of us to distinguish this difference.

Other people around us are commonly looking out for our welfare. They do so because they've learned to care for us. Our parents want nothing but the best for their children. Friends enjoy our company and don't like to see us get hurt. Co-workers give us advice from time to time and it's usually well-meaning. Other family members encourage us and regularly wish us well.

I equate the external input we receive from others to the 'sounds' factor explained above. It's the 'seems' factor which triggers our internal input and enables us to learn to feel certain things. We need to always remain cognizant of the inherent weaknesses associated with well-meaning, external input. This may try to lead us to water, but fortunately, it can't make us drink it.

Julie and I hadn't separated since the first time we met on August 14, 1987. We had been enjoying each other's company and seemed to appreciate how comfortably our relationship was moving along. After getting home from work one Friday, I walked to the mailbox to check for that day's mail. This was about two months or so after our first date. Here was a letter from Julie. I looked forward to reading it. I sat down on the couch and proceeded to do so.

Gary and Julie at Doug and Shirley's cottage.

This letter was very clear in its content. She was enjoying the fact that we were getting along well, but she was getting scared too. Julie expressed that it may be best if we slowed things down a bit. She was afraid of getting hurt again. This wasn't that long after her troubling divorce had become final. It had formally concluded at the end of August. She did not want to make a mistake by rushing into something that she would regret later; like our clearly advancing relationship.

You see, she had been getting considerable, well-meaning advice from others. Her mother could not believe that she'd responded to my personals ad, especially considering the fact that she was still recuperating from the end of a stressful marriage. Julie had been married for four years. As I got to know her, she definitely was not the type of person who would normally answer a personals ad in the newspaper. Correspondingly, I was not the type of person who'd normally write one either. Being more of an extrovert by nature, I typically meet people pretty easily.

Her well-meaning, best friend Pam had been cautioning her to be more careful. After all, the kind of guy she was likely to meet in a personals ad was not the type of guy you'd want to get involved with. Here I was, a 34-year-old bachelor who'd never been married. There must be some issues there which account for that. If he's that worthwhile, why is he still single? I still liked going out to the bars, attending band concerts and listening to rock music. This was not the type of person for her friend Julie. Pam and I had never met or talked though.

A co-worker named Marge had played bridge with a prior boss of mine and his wife. He was the least insecure boss that I ever worked for and we got along extremely well. He was aware of the fact that I'd previously called off a wedding on the night before it was to take place. This occurred before he'd hired me in October of 1983. The wedding was called off in February of 1981. When I worked for him I was a highly discretionary and cautious bachelor, but liked going out to the bars. Bob called me 'GB' and wrote me the nicest referral letter after I turned in my letter of resignation in March of 1985. I had accepted a different job that was located here in Oshkosh. When Marge heard that I'd called off a wedding at such a time, still liked going out and 'partying' a bit and hung out regularly with similar friends on the weekends, she had more than a strong enough case to identify me as a mid-thirties "playboy", bachelor type. She warned Julie to be careful and that it was probably best if she stayed away from me.

She was being filled with well-meaning, but very negative, advice from the people she was interacting and communicating with. I didn't stand a chance if this was my jury. They didn't even know me, but they were strongly cautioning her to slow things down, if not break this off, before she'd get badly hurt. After all, I must be commitment phobic, too.

I needed to go into work that upcoming Saturday morning and was an absolute basket case while there. Others could detect this too. I closed my door and had a good cry. I also had been hurt deeply by a previous relationship. Julie's letter triggered a very strong, handwritten rebuttal letter from me. My point was that not everything happens exactly when we want it to, but that it's those who best recognize things for what they truly are that will be the happiest in life and those that don't may be missing out on something that is truly special.

I'm the type of person who, when he feels comfortable, prefers to be very open. This was despite the fact that I was a bit jaded from the break up of my first serious relationship. I had been very candid with Julie. I basically let myself be fully open to her. In the letter I stressed that she was not the only one who stood to potentially get hurt here. A healthy relationship is one where both people are open, honest and truthful with each other. After reading her letter, I was bothered by the thought that I would now be pulling in and that this alone would hamper the future of our relationship. I expressed that to her as well. My response to Julie flowed very easily from my heart.

Thankfully, we both recognized that we were involved with something very special. We didn't consciously slow things down, but rather proceeded to move steadily forward in appreciation of our lives together. We dated each other exclusively and spent considerable time getting to know one another. We've never lost sight of the fact that we are extremely compatible. Then on Valentine's Day 1988, we got engaged. Julie had totally moved in with me, in my home, by the end of that summer. We got married on October 1st of that year. We've not been emotionally apart since the ATTENTION GETTING LETTER received on that Friday in October of 1987 was addressed. Thankfully, it 'seemed' to be the right thing to do.

Julie and Gary relaxing on a couch.

‧ 18 ‧
And IN THE GARDEN
IT WILL BE...But Wait

There are numerous external forces which impact our ability to meet someone special to share our lives with. It's extremely difficult to find that workable match because the word 'workable' needs to take so many complex things into consideration. Anyone's efforts to 'find that perfect match' will likely be detoured somewhere along the way.

"In this world of uncertainty and confusion, we two have found each other... different yet alike. We have grown together in love and understanding." These are the exact same words that are written on the front of our carefully chosen wedding invitation. We believed it best said how we felt back then. These exact words would still apply today if Julie and I were asked to describe our 25-year marriage.

The important thing for each of us to realize is that we don't need the perfect match to be perfectly happy in our lives. I didn't say content, I said perfectly happy. Content sounds too much like the equivalent of satisficing. I'm not into satisficing when it comes to closely sharing my life together with someone. I expect much more than that, but I didn't strive for the perfect match because I'm not sure it even truly exists. How would you go about defining it? Thankfully, we are all different people, both scientifically and practically.

When we talked about where we would like to be married, we considered a number of things. Julie had been married before and wanted to be considerate of that fact. I had come extremely close to being married once, calling the wedding off the Friday night before it was to take place. Neither of us had children from previous relationships. We both had very small immediate families. Julie's parents were alive and she had one younger brother named Matt. My father had passed away when I was 18, but my mother was thankfully still alive. I also only had the one brother, Doug, who was married over 35 years to Shirley.

Once we informed our family, it was time to ask Doug to be my Best Man and Shirley to be Julie's Matron of Honor. They couldn't have been happier for us and were most proud to accept. Our parents and Matt were very happy, too. When you have a small family, you especially treasure such moments and times.

Julie had previously been married in the Catholic church. I had expected to be married there. We arranged an appointment to meet with the priest at St. Raphael's Catholic church here on the westside of Oshkosh to discuss the potential for us to get married in this church. We told him that we would be honored to do so and would welcome the opportunity to become new members there. Once Julie and I listened to what was required by the Catholic church in order for this to take place, we were not interested. Any attempt to disavow that her first marriage had taken place seemed sacrilegious to us. We're both very strong principles people. We also would have had to pay good money to have this process take place. We respect the primary intentions and beliefs of any person associated with the various Christian faiths (and for that matter, the freedom others have to practice any of their respective faiths). We politely told the priest that we would no longer be interested in getting married in his church.

My mother and Aunt Phyllis were active church goers. I was raised in the Episcopalian faith and went to church regularly as a child. My Aunt worked tirelessly, for many years, on the altar guild at the beautiful Episcopalian church here in town. We arranged to meet with her young pastor there. She had told him about our intended marriage and that we'd be getting in contact with him shortly regarding the possibility of getting married in his church. I arranged such an appointment and we were shocked by the indignity we were given during our conversation with him. There was another money catch involved with his willingness to cooperate with us. We were even more turned off by his ambivalence. My aunt was pretty upset by this; she wasn't mad at us, but was very disappointed to learn what had transpired.

We then considered other options. It became clear to us that we would likely not be getting married in a traditional church setting. That was okay. Our faith was deeper than that. We, thankfully, approached the curator involved with an absolutely beautiful and historic facility here in town. It is known as the Paine Art Center and Gardens. It is formally recognized as one of the last great castles still standing in this country. They feature numerous outdoor garden settings and it seemed to be the perfect place for us to hold our wedding. Their Formal Garden was magnificent and it was clearly our location of choice. Most importantly, it was available to us on Saturday, October 1, 1988.

Fortunately we were recommended, by my Aunt Phyllis, to talk with Father Elmer Harvey. He was a retired Methodist minister.

This was the encouraged alternative spot for our wedding just shortly before it was to actually take place (Julie's Mom is in the foreground).

What a wonderful person! We were very impressed after having a meeting with him...within his former church; which, ironically, is located very near to the steel-gated Paine complex. We've found our spiritual beliefs to be less compatible with conventional religion. These beliefs are extremely strong and run very deep within us, but we respect the rights of others to express their own beliefs as well. Father Harvey was a very well-respected person in our community and we could understand why. He could tell that we were very much in love and was honored to be able to join the two of us in marriage. How refreshing this was after our earlier conversations with the two other men of God.

The Formal Garden at the Paine prior to their actual wedding in 1988.

I was still bothered by the fact that the defined attendants and ushers in my 'anticipated' first wedding were left with the expense of rented tuxes and purchased dresses. It was important to us to at least recognize some special honor attendants in the program of our wedding. Julie asked her best friend Pam to be so honored as well. She respectfully declined. This hurt Julie quite a bit because Pam had stood up in her first wedding and Julie later stood up in Pam's. It was quite apparent that Pam did not support Julie and I getting married at this time.

On the morning of October 1, 1988, it was quite overcast and rainy. The forecast wasn't that disruptive. It sounded like the showers were to back off considerably by late morning/early afternoon. As we were getting ready, we were concerned about the weather with the ceremony being held outside.

I was staying positive, but by the time we got over to the Paine it was still raining enough to use an umbrella. It had definitely lightened up quite a bit as we were getting closer to the time of the actual wedding service.

Shortly before we were going to be heading out to the Formal Garden, the staff at the Paine was encouraging us to move our ceremony to a different place. This location was much smaller and we'd have been getting married under a concrete canopy that was an actual structural part of the building's southeast corner. A large number of our guests had already entered, positioned themselves and were awaiting our appearance. This Garden

We're Only Just Beginning . . .

Saturday, October 1, 1988
The Formal Garden
Paine Art Center & Arboretum
Rev. Elmer L. Harvey Officiating

The Marriage of
Julie Ann Lemke and Gary Lee Beyer

Best Man: Douglas J. Beyer
the brother of the groom

Matron of Honor: Shirley C. Beyer
the sister-in-law of the groom

Usher: Matthew J. Lemke
the brother of the bride

Parents of the Bride: Joan and William Lemke

Parents of the Groom: Grace and (the late) Clarence Beyer

Honor Attendants: (friends of the groom)

Randy Bondow	Paul Steger
Gene Langenecker	Gary West
Gary Ludwig	Randy Wild
Timothy Pagel	

. . . This certainly is the happiest day of our lives

Our wedding handout.

was about a hundred feet further back in the far east side of the complex. This would have severely dampened (please pardon the pun) most everything we had hoped for in the ceremony. We had two singers ready to go, that were former students of Julie. There were mikes and speakers already in place. In the location they wanted us to move to, there was no electrical service. The guests would have had to stand out in potential rain anyway and their visibility to us would been much more limited and restricted. It just made no sense. Thankfully, we held our ground and our much anticipated outdoor wedding was wonderful. Shortly into the service, most of the umbrellas were closed and they were kept closed for the remainder of it.

I got pretty choked up and had a hard time getting out some of the words during the ceremony. When it comes down to it, I'm a very sensitive person. This was extremely emotional for me and any tears I shed were tears of absolute joy and appreciation. I was feeling very fortunate. The featured song in our wedding was "Endless Love" sung by Lionel Richie and Diana Ross. My mother had gotten pretty sick a few days before the wedding and had lost a fair amount of weight. I believe it was strictly caused by nerves. After my earlier close call, she was probably reliving some of the trauma involved. Who could blame her.

We had a large turnout and there were people there we hadn't seen in awhile. It was great to see Julie's best friend Pam and her husband Dana in attendance. Matt did a much appreciated job keeping everything moving nicely and helping people become comfortable. After the service we gathered for pictures. These pictures actually turned out wonderful with the type of sky we had for a background that day. Getting the sun in our eyes

Gary and Julie in the horse-drawn carriage that was a complete surprise from his Mom.

was not an issue and from looking at most of the pictures, one wouldn't have guessed the type of day it was.

My Mom surprised us with a wonderful horse-drawn carriage. This showed up right at the end of the service. She couldn't have gotten us a neater surprise. That was Mom though; she loved doing stuff like this. Rodger, from Cavanaugh's Carriages in Neenah gave us a ride across town to the place where our reception was to be held. This was a considerable trip for a horse-drawn carriage. Shortly after leaving the complex we went over a bridge. The cars were honking, and we were smiling.

We later received a $100 charge from The Paine for stepping down their grass. This charge came weeks after our wedding was over. You could call this a real Paine in arrears…just some weak accounting humor, sorry! We'll always fondly remember this awesome day and our wonderful wedding ceremony at the Paine. Julie and I have never been viewed as your typical high school teacher and accountant. Our atypical wedding day story seems most appropriate as well. No one there will ever forget that it was IN THE (Formal) GARDEN where it actually took place; that first day of October in 1988.

The new man and wife.

୧ 19 ଔ
THE EVENING ACCOUNTING TEACHER At His Alma Mater

I'd been working in the corporate accounting world for a number of years. It was the summer of 1990. I was working as Plant Controller at Morgan Manufacturing here in Oshkosh. I had previously expressed an interest in teaching an evening accounting class. My wife had been a high school teacher for a number of years and I thought that I might enjoy the challenge of doing this, as well as bringing a different perspective into the classroom.

I received a telephone call from Bill Zorr, a past accounting professor of mine. He called to inquire if I'd be interested in teaching an evening class in Managerial Accounting at the University of Wisconsin-Oshkosh for the Fall Semester of the 1989-90 school year.

During my high school years, my Dad had experienced some pretty significant health problems. He had suffered a heart attack prior to this time and this was before open heart surgery procedures were very common. I can remember him needing to take nitroglycerin tablets under his tongue after some scary episodes as I was growing up. He was diagnosed with colon cancer and after major surgery, he ended up with a colostomy. I'll never forget my father lying spread out on the radiant heat floor of our carpeted living room to alleviate relentless, cramping pains. Tears would run down his face, but he never complained. He had a hobby of making custom lamps and fixtures. It's truly sad and unfortunate that he only lived a couple of weeks past his retirement. He was a person who loved life and he would not have just gone off into the sunset to lick his wounds.

I was a good student in high school who spent a fair amount of time in hospitals as my Dad spent considerable time in and out of them throughout this period. My wonderful mother was never one to complain either. She was always there to help both of us. I always liked math and did well in it. My only brother, Doug, encouraged me to pursue accounting in college. He worked in an office for over 25 years. From what he'd seen, he believed accounting would be perfect for me because it mixed in math with a solid profession that most companies relied on. The pay in this field was good as well.

I had pretty much made up my mind that I was going to pursue an accounting degree in college. My Dad passed away on August 3rd, and classes were beginning in September. I stayed the course and proceeded to follow the recommended path for getting through school in four years. In my sophomore year I had my first accounting class. Debits and credits were the pulse of my days. The second class, in cost accounting, was a bit more interesting because tangible products, people and machinery entered the picture. Next, it was time for the start of the upper level courses. The intent was that most of the non-serious accounting types would have been weeded out by this point.

It is then when I first met accounting professor Bill Zorr. I had him for Advanced Accounting I and he was a good teacher. He had a nice class presence and a very quick wit. However, he was no nonsense. His tests were an absolute bear and he expected strong performance from his students. I ended up with a B in his class and was bummed. My grade was so close to an A, but it didn't matter in the end. When I went to talk with him in his office, he told me that there were only three As in the class and that I'd gotten the highest B. I remember asking him, "couldn't I have the lowest A?" The next semester I had Zorr for Advanced Accounting II. I believe he knew that I was serious about pursuing a career in accounting. I had longer hair back then and didn't fit the image of the typical accountant, but it wouldn't have taken long to tell that I was serious about it if someone took the time to look beyond the surface. Bill Zorr was intelligent and in tune. The very first day of this class he caught me prior to leaving and we had a brief conversation that I will never forget. He basically said, this time if you're on the cusp, I'll give you the benefit of the doubt. That definitely did not sit well with me and I believe he knew it. I didn't want anybody to give me anything like that. I deserved to get what I had earned.

I ended up getting a B in this class and went on to earn my undergraduate degree in accounting in May of 1975. I went through various on campus interviews, but was not really the right type of person to go into public accounting. My father and brother worked for many years in the foundry industry. I liked the idea that industrial accounting offered me the opportunity to work with a wide array of people who filled diverse roles within a company. A management-based accountant would work closely with marketing, inventory control, the shop floor, sales, human resources and the other important functions which were necessary to operate a larger business. I was always more of an extrovert (which certainly never fit the image of the typical accountant).

I accepted a job offer from a company whose Corporate headquarters was in Green Bay. This started with an on-campus interview. I later went on to get my MBA in accounting and finance. As the years went on, I'd commonly have people tell me that I didn't seem like an accountant. Others, including friends, would say, "Gar, don't take it the wrong way, but you don't come across as the typical accountant." I always took this as a compliment and always will. I have a solid reputation and earned the respect of co-workers, at all levels, who got to know me. My integrity has and always will be extremely important to me.

I had gotten very involved in a professional support group called the Institute of Management Accountants (aka IMA). I held chapter positions of Secretary and Vice President of Membership and Marketing. I took this seriously and in the latter position was able to bring in some pretty impressive and noteworthy speakers during my one-year term. Bill Zorr was extremely active in IMA and was a past President. In conversations I'd had with Bill, I expressed my interest in possibly teaching an evening accounting class, in an adjunct capacity, and asked him if he would please keep me in

my mind if a situation presented itself.

In addition to Zorr, two other of my past accounting professors (Mr.'s Ostendorf and McKay) were also going

UW-Oshkosh College of Business.

The centennial pin.

to be teaching this same class during the day. When Bill asked if I would be interested in teaching the evening version, I was extremely honored. To be asked to teach a class that is reflective of your major at your alma mater was pretty neat. I actually have a lot of respect for Bill Zorr; as I do have for Harry Ostendorf and Duane McKay. The UW-Oshkosh accounting program has long been recognized as one of the top programs in the country.

Zorr was to have exclusive input into the exams for this course and we were not to see them prior to passing them out. There were a total of 35 students in my class and I ended up receiving some very strong positive and reinforcing feedback from them. I'm proud of this fact as well. There was an interesting complication which occurred during the semester. My background was quite solid in manufacturing accounting and I had the opportunity to learn from some good and some bad ideas. One bad idea is called the sales value approach to the assigning of product costs. This was identified as an option in the class text and I made it very clear during class that this option should never be used to determine product costs. It will only get one in trouble because the basis for such assignment is totally inappropriate, let alone highly inaccurate. You probably have already guessed this. The infamous sales value approach to assigning costs appeared in a test question on one of the three major exams which involved an actual calculation of such costs. The concept was simple to understand and the calculation was quite easy, but some students freaked when they saw it on the exam.

Teaching this class was both enjoyable and professionally rewarding. It is an experience I will always think back on fondly and never regret. However, combining this with a demanding full-time, accounting management job was just too much. I've been asked would I ever consider doing this full-time. My answer is "no" because I do not believe I'm the right type of person for doing this year after year. At least for one special semester I can proudly say that I was THE EVENING ACCOUNTING TEACHER at his alma mater.

THE EVENING ACCOUNTING TEACHER At His Alma Mater

The following statements were copied from the blue response forms used in conducting the <u>Survey of Student Opinion of Instruction and Courses</u> in your class. The statements are typed exactly as they were written by the students.

<u>NAME</u>	<u>DEPT/COURSE/SECTION</u>	<u>DATE</u>
GARY BEYER	28-202-008	11-09-89

Instructor did a tremendous job on making material informative and pertinent. He has a greater skill in teaching than I have experienced from prof's in affiliated courses.

Best instructor I ever had. He respects students and understands them. I also think that he cares about us learning and is very devoted.

Tests in class not 2 1/2 hrs cannot remember enough studying 5 chapters.

I think Gary is an excellent teacher and I wish we could have normal class hours to get more in depth rather than cramming it all in.

Gary is an excellent instructor. He shows us the "real world" examples applicable to the course-work. I would <u>HIGHLY</u> recommend to students!

It is good how you relate it to everyday life, but I would like you to use more examples outside of the problems.

Partial student feedback from class I taught.

You Must Answer This

๛ 20 ๛
January 1st, 1993...BRRRR

We had a quiet New Year's Eve. 1992 had been an exhausting year for us and it seemed appropriate to have it go out like a lamb. Each New Year's Day, a local furniture store that we liked had a major sale. Regardless if we ended up buying anything or not; we always enjoyed checking it out. It was kind of a nice way to start the New Year. When we got up it was cold, and we decided to drive around the subdivision a bit to warm up the car. We had no specific route in mind. There was a new subdivision being developed to our immediate north and we took a left turn onto Greenfield Trail which would pass through it.

We were making small talk and reached a third intersection. Julie and I each looked to the west and saw this gorgeous house at the end of a cul de sac there. It was bordered in the back by this impressive wood line. It was love at first sight. We turned left, pulled in the driveway, got out of our car and walked around the home.

We were not actively looking to change homes. However, we had gotten frustrated with our existing place and were open to making a change. I'd purchased this home prior to meeting Julie. It still had nice curb appeal, but there were some issues with it that bothered us.

I've always enjoyed having a real Christmas tree in the home. I believed it was the way it was meant to be. Decorating the tree was something I always looked forward to each Holiday season. It was not a chore for me. We had accumulated a number of nice ornaments over the years and the finished product usually was pretty cool. I especially liked trimming Fraser firs and would commonly get a taller tree. There were only a couple of choices we had for locating it.

There was a dining room-type area in this home and we were not that formal. Other than in our living room, everything always seemed pretty tight. There was this very small area which jutted out from a corner of the living room. We'd put a portable fireplace and larger artificial plant here, but it was crowded looking. One year, we decided to try to put our Christmas tree in this spot. It was so cramped. I remember telling Julie that this was ridiculous.

We decided to see what it would cost to remove the back wall of this area and create an opening between the dining and living rooms. This really turned out nice. We ended up adding a two-level deck to the back of the home and incorporated a sliding door on the west wall of this dining room. It brought much more light into the house and the layout became much more functional for us.

Regardless of the improvements made, there were just some things that still bothered us. We lived in a nice neighborhood and appreciated the quick access to the highway for Julie's job. The city's Westside was developing nicely and had become an attractive place to live. Over the prior two to three years we'd lived in the home, we began going to some open houses and the annual Parade of Homes tours. We had created a mindset that if the right thing would come along; we were open to looking into it.

When we saw this home on Golden Avenue, it definitely got our attention. It was one of only two completed homes, not only in the cul de sac, but on the entire side of the street. The driveway was clear, but there was snow on the ground. We didn't have boots on, however, it didn't matter. There were no blinds or curtains on any of the windows, so we were able to look inside.

Our floor-to-ceiling fireplace.

When we looked into the large three window with circle top scheme at the front of the home, we saw this beautiful brick floor to ceiling fireplace. It stole the show! The home's exterior and interior colors, as well as its features, really appealed to us.

The fact that it was by this extensive, wooded area stood out for both of us.

This was something that Julie would have ranked high in a list of preferred items. Her parents lived by a lake in a heavily wooded area and she was able to appreciate the benefits from this. What we didn't realize until later, was that the woods were in a protected zone whereby other homes would not be able to be built where it stood. Therefore, this offered the best of both worlds. There would be significant, ongoing privacy, yet there would be the seasonal benefits associated with this beautiful woods.

There was a post with a realtor's sign in the front yard. We saw this when we first looked into the cul de sac. Julie wrote down her name and telephone number and we headed back home to make a call. Her name was Jean Petts and she answered the phone. We told her what had happened and she promptly said, "would you like to go through it today?" On this very cold New Year's Day, she drove in from 60 miles north of us to show us the inside. Jean was probably in her mid-60s at the time, but clearly was a real mover and shaker. It's little wonder that she was such a high producer and was well-respected in her field. She even left her own New Year's party to show us this home. I'm sure she could tell from the excitement in our voices that we were legitimate prospects for potentially purchasing it.

It only got better when we went through the home. We were pretty fussy, but it was convincing. It turned out that there already was a conditional offer to purchase that had been written on this property. It had been a Parade Home in the summer of 1992; it's ironic that we hadn't seen it. I had been pretty busy with work and I don't believe we checked into any of the Parade Homes during this time. The fact that we headed to our north on that cold Friday morning of January 1st was no coincidence. We ended up writing an unconditional offer on the home that very afternoon. The people who placed the conditional offer were given appropriate time to convert their offer over to an unconditional one. Thankfully for us, they weren't able to swing it at that time.

Next came the need for us to make some arrangements. We certainly weren't in a position to carry mortgages on two homes. We were able to secure a short-term bridge loan from the equity we had in our existing one. We then quickly listed it for sale. By the grace of God, we received an unconditional offer on the house not long thereafter. Its sale was closed in early March.

I'd been very busy with normal year-end closing responsibilities at work. Time went very fast; it seemed like a whirlwind. We settled into the home on February 23rd. Our families helped us considerably with the efforts associated with leaving the old home and moving into our new one. We'd had a beautiful, "portable" oak bar in our other home. We were able to feature it in the basement of the new one and also incorporate some supportive living space.

I always wanted a sun room and the western exposure of this home made it appealing to do so. We had this added on by the original builder in 1996. Thankfully, I came home early one afternoon to check on its progress. The workers had the studwork up for the room. Their height looked too short to me and I questioned one of the guys about it. Fortunately I did, because if left the way it was, the ceiling height of the room would have been wrong, the window sizes would have been too small and the room definitely would not have been acceptable to us. He told me to get in touch with the builder as soon as possible, which I attempted to do. There were some mistakes being made and some incorrect assumptions were involved. We got them satisfactorily resolved and the wonderful sunroom was completed in mid-October.

On May 12, 2000, we were significantly impacted by a major hail storm which blasted our area. We needed to replace both our shingles and our siding. When the sunroom was added, they were able to match the siding, but were not able to match the shingles which were on the rest of the home. Even the siding work didn't match that well and it looked like the room had been added on. In conjunction with the associated repair and replacement work, the sunroom now looked like it was part of the original construction.

In June of 2001, another major storm hit our area with sixty miles per hour winds. A large burr oak just missed hitting a corner of our sunroom and the northwest corner of our lot experienced the loss of a significant number of larger-sized trees. There was a silver lining though in that this storm cleared out what's become an attractive cove-like area in our backyard. It's another example of where something which was bad inadvertently created something which became good.

We never did get to our intended destination of the furniture store on January of 1993. What led us to drive around was the extremely cold weather on that day. There are a lot of different options to drive within this area of the city of Oshkosh. One would most commonly head to the south or west and be able to drive for quite some time. Heading to the east will shortly involve crossing over a highway and offers a less suburban feel. We were meant to head north on the morning of JANUARY 1, 1993, and drive into the highly undeveloped area. Despite the associated BRRRR, we thankfully saw something which has dramatically enhanced our lives for the last 20-plus years. It was our dream home!

The front of the house.

You Must Answer This

‏❧ 21 ❧
Your Position Is
BEING ELIMINATED

It was the fall of 1993; the weather was beautiful and we were getting closer to Halloween. We'd purchased a brand new home in February that bordered a wood line and the leaves were changing over to some awesome looking colors. On Friday morning, October 11th, I received a telephone call from my boss saying, "Gary, can you please stop down to my office?" At this time my office was on the third floor and I proceeded to head downstairs to his which was on the first floor. Sitting inside were my boss Paul, the Director of Plant Operations, and the Manufacturing Division Human Resources Director whose name was Bruce. Paul asked me to sit down and I was told that the company's Manufacturing Division was quietly, but actively, being put up for sale. He is the person who'd originally hired me when he was in the role of Plant Controller.

I was presented with two options; one was for me to be kept on until a sale was completed whereby I would discriminately become part of a data communications team for potential buyers, the second option was for my Plant Controller position to be eliminated/absorbed immediately. I was then told, "We need your decision by Monday." This had to be faced and dealt with and it was totally unexpected.

This story actually begins in the fall of 1983. I had been working for a division of Medalist Industries in Berlin, Wisconsin for the previous five years. The division was called Sand-Knit and they had gained the prestigious reputation of being "The Designer For The Pros." Here in this very small town, athletic uniforms were designed and manufactured for most of the NFL teams, most of the NBA teams, most of the major college and university teams and a handful of MLB teams. Because I am a huge sports fan, this work environment was very appealing to me. I was hired for the position of Assistant Controller and was not looking to change jobs.

I would periodically be contacted by professional recruiters regarding my interest level in checking out various positions which would open up around the Fox River Valley area of Wisconsin. A recruiter called me in October of 1983 regarding a Cost Accounting Manager's position with a larger company in Fond du Lac, Wisconsin. At this time, I was living in my own home in Oshkosh and was driving about twenty five miles to work every day. She told me about the position and its associated compensation and I told her that I was open to checking it out. Shortly thereafter, I received a call and she said the person that would be my boss was wondering if I could meet with him at Nino's Steakhouse in Oshkosh early that same evening for an interview and meal. I agreed, and ended up being offered the position. I accepted it prior to the completion of our meeting.

My drive to Fond du Lac was pretty much equivalent to my drive to Berlin. This company was involved with the manufacturing of automotive ignition parts and accessories for sale to after market suppliers. It was a far cry from the manufacturing and sale of athletic wear. The company had experienced some significant inventory control related issues and were being consistently surprised by hits associated with their annual physical inventories. The position was challenging, and I always liked that, but I also felt a ton of pressure. My boss was outstanding. He was probably the least insecure person I've ever worked for. I tried very hard to identify and implement various benchmarking-type controls to help me gauge and track actual performance. They had about a $22 million dollar inventory at the time, so even a one percent hit would be over $200,000. The results of the subsequent physical inventory came back with a small gain which is what you would prefer. I was extremely relieved and so was everyone else involved.

In March of 1985, I was contacted by a different recruiter, whose name was Katy Rodon. She asked of my interest in another Cost Accounting Manager's position. This one was with a company located right in Oshkosh and it was recognized as the leading wood door manufacturer in the country. I was reluctant to pursue it because I'd recently been professionally satisfied and personally pleased by the outcomes of my efforts at the company in Fond du Lac. She was a persistent recruiter and had contacted me a number of times telling me that I should at least interview for this opening or I might kick myself later.

I agreed to an after work interview and was to meet with a gentleman named Paul Case, who was the Plant Controller and would become my boss. I liked Paul and a short time later ended up being offered the position. However, I decided to turn it down. I'll never forget a follow up call I received from Katy on a Saturday morning. She said that they were really interested in me and wanted to set up another interview, this time with the corporation's Chief Financial Officer. This was on a Thursday, after work, and on my way driving there, I told myself that this would be it. There'd be no wishy-washy decision making involved. I'd made up my mind in advance that it would either be a definite "yes" or a definite "no." The CFO, Mike Lupo, was an intimidating person. He was tall, forthright and incredibly blunt.

I accepted the position, but there was a bit of a conflict with the timing. Being a huge fan of Milwaukee Brewers baseball, I had gotten tickets for their upcoming home opener. This was one of my very favorite things to do and I always looked forward to this annual right of spring. I was brought in for a meeting with some of their accounting management and MIS staff before I was to officially begin my employment with them. There was to be some software training held in New Orleans that they wanted me to attend as a substitute for one of the managers who couldn't make it. This got dicey because the final day of this training was the day before the date of the game I was committed to attending. There was supposed to be a big appreciation party associated with this training that would definitely conflict with my getting to the game. The accounting manager Mike Morrissey, who I was to substitute for, took my part and I'll never forget that. I ended up flying back the evening that the training had finished and was happily able to attend the game in Milwaukee the next day.

Over my nine plus years of employment with the door manufacturer, Morgan Products Limited, I had the opportunity to grow in a number of different ways. I was promoted from Cost Accounting Manager to the position of Plant Controller. I was able to earn the respect of plant, manufacturing division and Corporate staff. I am very proud of the fact that "In summary, I believe the Oshkosh facility has the best Controller in the entire Manufacturing Group" was written at the very end of my 1989 performance review by Paul Case, for whom I have a great deal of respect. The Oshkosh plant was by far the largest of their four wood door

Gary at work at Morgan Products.

manufacturing plants. I was asked to travel to two of their other plants in Springfield, Oregon, and Lexington, North Carolina, while I was there. These trips were intended to provide some internal consulting-type advice to their plant's management. Before they agreed to purchase a small hardwoods plant in Shawano, Wisconsin, and a number of times thereafter, I was asked for my input regarding this facility. They directed me to become familiar with its operation and to identify a reliable performance measurement and reporting system for them. For awhile, I spent one to two days per week there and monthly inventories were taken. Later, we hired an on-site accounting manager who had indirect reporting responsibility to myself. There came a time when I was selected, along with a handful of people, to visit and survey a Premdor manufacturing plant in Canada to help with the determination of a proper valuation of this company's assets prior to its potential acquisition.

In the summer of 1990 or 1991, I received an early morning call from my boss at the time, Paul Case. This was at about 4:30 a.m. He said "Gary, you needn't come into work this morning. We incurred a major fire last night and your office area was hit pretty hard. There was an issue with the plant's spark arrestor system." Needless to say, I wasn't going back to sleep. Paul was calling me from onsite and I told him that I would get ready and come over shortly. My office at this time was on the third floor, above plant operations. When I got there, it was clear that the fire was caused by an explosion. Representatives from the fire department allowed me to climb the stairs to survey the damage. I couldn't believe my eyes when I walked into what was left of the accounting department. It looked like a heavily hit combat zone! My office looked like a grenade had been tossed into it. There was little doubt in anyone's mind that if this would have taken place during normal business hours, there would have been some serious injuries involved, if not casualties. The odds of the explosion occurring when it did were considerably less than during the day when door production was at its peak and much more sawdust was being generated throughout the plant. There was only a skeleton crew at work during this disruption, and thankfully, there were no injuries. By the grace of God, my staff and I were not meant to be there when this took place. My wife has said many times that she almost became a widow that day. Plant accounting was temporarily relocated to a make-do location until a more permanent solution could be arrived at. In the course of my employment there, I was probably transplanted a half a dozen different times.

Door production, at one point, represented about 75 percent of the company's business. The remaining 25 percent was attributable to the design and manufacture of stair parts. This was a considerably higher margin portion of their business, but the associated margins were consistently taking a hit. The responsible product managers were regularly hearing complaints from distributors in the marketplace that product pricing had to be lowered in order for them to increase sales. There was constant pressure to decrease prices and this challenge was satisfied by a steady reduction in such prices. It reached a point where stair part margins, although still much higher than net door margins, had become unacceptable to upper management.

Stair parts were manufactured in house and were responsible for a good deal of overhead absorption/coverage. Some of this absorption was unobvious to many, but I was able to define it and consistently tried to both communicate and defend this fact. I distinctly remember a stressful conversation that I had with the Stair Parts Plant Manager when he brusquely told me, "Gary, I cannot satisfy quality, delivery requirements and cost control at the same time." His area had been experiencing considerable levels of overtime. A major meeting to discuss the status of our stair parts business was scheduled one morning. I'll never forget it. Herm Mollenkopf was my well-seasoned and highly capable boss at this time. He was the Director of Plant Operations. He and I headed over to this meeting which was to be held in the Manufacturing Division offices. They were located just across the street from us. It was clear that the decision to discontinue this part of the business had already been made. We walked back to our offices and were just shaking our heads. From this point on, the company seemed to steadily deteriorate with regard to performance. The products were good, but the incessant pressures from the marketplace became too much to satisfactorily overcome.

I've learned firsthand how fickle various corporate environments can become. I distinctly remember, quite ridiculously, busting my tail to meet an unrealistic budget-related deadline. I incurred hurt feelings by missing a family wedding reception because I was intently finishing a meticulously prepared plant budget package. I was very proud of it and so was our team. We made the deadline only to find out that the deadline was then significantly moved because the other three smaller plants were not able to achieve it: talk about disheartening! I've seen my share of artificial deadlines, there's not much worse in working environments when you take what you do seriously.

It's interesting how, at one time, you're considered invaluable and at another time you're determined to be expendable. I used to frequently get calls directly from the President of the Manufacturing Division. He would ask me some very hypothetical questions and ask for my advice on certain subjects. I initially took this as a compliment, but it became very uncomfortable for me because it caused me to be put in some pretty awkward positions. A person's perception, especially as it relates to co-workers, can impair their view of reality. It's very frustrating when you find yourself inadvertently caught between a rock and a hard place. Other people's insecurities can certainly come into play and this can cause what were otherwise, non-existent problems in your life. Answering to multiple bosses can be difficult too.

When Julie and I discussed the two options that were presented to me on that October morning, I found her support to be incredible. I've never been a phony and she knew, like I did, that I had no interest in playing an artificial role while the company was being positioned for sale. Fortunately, she had a reliable job which she liked and this gave us the opportunity to turn down their primary offer. A severance package was given to me through the end of the year and outplacement services were also provided. My situation was part of a larger, belt-tightening directive that was intended to make the division appear more attractive and streamlined for the purpose of its sale. It also featured the elimination of other manufacturing division management and staff positions. We were later to learn, during an evening of dining with former CFO Mike Lupo and his wife, that my decision to not accept their offer, but rather choosing to accept my immediate termination, had definitely taken them by surprise. I do not know how Mike was able to find this out, but he told this to me unequivocally that evening.

The important point here is, despite the despair normally being associated with the phrase, "your position is BEING ELIMINATED," one must always remain true to themselves. Your integrity and what you stand for can never be taken from you if you don't let it. Morgan Products had been an excellent place for me to work for many years. I gained some wonderful experience there and will always look back on it with good feelings. I had the pleasure of working with some outstanding people, a number of whom I still consider to be friends. Many things can force us to make changes in our lives. We can't hide from them and it's best when we identify them for what they are. Most importantly, we must effectively handle them because they will impact how and what we do.

You Must Answer This

‭෴ 22 ෴‬
It Was Shortly Before Turning 30 and Then, NOT LONG AFTER TURNING 60

The Milwaukee Brewers played in their first and only World Series in the fall of 1982. I had never been to Spring Training before and March of 1983 was clearly the time for me to go. Among other things, I really hoped to meet and talk with Brewers player Charlie Moore. This was because both he and I were going to be turning 30 on June 21st of that year. I'd already checked and the team was to be playing the Red Sox in Boston on that day and I wanted to mention this to Charlie. Well, not only did we talk, my mother took a picture of us standing next to each other. How cool is that?

I had this picture developed into 5 x7 and 8x10 photos to be proudly displayed in my home, I'd never attempted to get them autographed. That is until Friday morning August 9, 2013. Both pictures were returned to me personalized and autographed on the following Thursday; less than one week from when I'd initiated my efforts to, hopefully, get this matter accomplished. What's very interesting is that we both turned 60 less than two months earlier. I'll explain...

I've been a huge major league baseball fan since I was a very young child. My Dad used to take me along to Milwaukee Braves games, so I saw some of the all-time greats play in Hank Aaron, Warren Spahn and Eddie Mathews. I used to play hide and seek in the yards with the neighbor kids and would give away my hiding spots by cheering too loud after a Braves player had done something good. This was because I typically kept a small transistor radio glued to my ear to listen to the games. Years later, I had the wonderful opportunity to tell long-time Braves radio announcer Earl Gillespie about this and recalled a specific time when Mack Jones hit a huge home run and I couldn't hold it in. He laughed and said "now there's a name from the past that I'd forgotten about."

My Dad never finished high school, but ended up becoming Core Room Superintendant over three plants for Neenah Foundry Company. One of the people who called on him periodically lived in Milwaukee and got to know that I just loved baseball. He would get us tickets for games from time to time. My Dad was 47 when I was born, but he never seemed to let the age difference stand in his way. After one Braves game, we later went to enjoy a nice meal at Ray Jackson's Supper Club on Bluemound (which was by the stadium). Dad's contact Ted was very familiar with it and I had my little white autograph book with me. I'd been sitting down when Ted called for Dad and I to go to the bar area. Here were Eddie Mathews and Johnny Logan sitting there having a cocktail. Logan had been playing in Japan and autographed my treasured book in Japanese. Many years later, in the bowels of old Milwaukee County Stadium, I was with my wife and able to repeat this story to him.

When the Braves left Wisconsin for Georgia in 1965, I was devastated. My parents purchased a powerful, multi-band radio for me, where I could listen to them play some evening games via an Atlanta station. I also used to enjoy listening to Harry Caray and Jack Buck do the play by play for St. Louis Cardinals games on KMOX. In 1970 the Seattle Pilots franchise was relocated to Milwaukee and was re-named the Brewers. They got a serious fan, right out of the blocks, in myself. Over the years I went to most of their home openers in Milwaukee. However, the years have been pretty lean performance wise.

In 1982 things were different. The team not only won the American League pennant but took the the reverent Cardinals to a seventh game in the World Series before losing 6-3. This was huge for any Brewers fan. Charlie Moore made an unforgettable play in the final game of the previous playoff series. The Angels were leading 3-2 in the bottom of the fifth inning

Johnny Logan autograph from May 2, 1965, at Ray Jackson's in Milwaukee.

and threatening to score more runs when Moore threw a straight-line dart to third base from his spot in right field to gun down a shocked Reggie Jackson who was heading from first to third after seeing a ball get through the infield for a base hit. The next hitter singled, which would have scored Jackson to make it 4-2 and keep the inning alive and well. Charlie also ended up scoring the Brewers tying run as they went on to win the game and their first ever pennant, 4-3. I was working for Medalist Sand-Knit at this time and they actually made the Brewers uniforms. In my position as Assistant Controller, I was able to get to know their Traveling Secretary Tommy Ferguson. What a great guy!! He definitely had a passion for the game of baseball.

My wonderful mother was always a good sport. She'd turned 71 in late February of 1983 and had never been on a larger plane flight. Ironically, she had been taken up once in a small, single engine plane over Milwaukee. I decided to go to Brewers Spring Training in Sun City, Arizona, around Christmas time. I asked my mother if she'd be interested in going along and she was more than willing. Tommy knew that I was a huge fan and he facilitated me being able to work through their trainer, Freddie Frederico. I communicated with Freddie and he arranged to get us tickets to see some Brewers games while we were there. I couldn't think of anything I'd sooner be doing. We left very early in the morning of Saturday, March 19, 1983. Renting a Datsun Sentra while there, we put over 900 miles on it. The beautiful weather and incomparable landscape supported our welcomed change of pace. We visited Phoenix and Tucson and took in Sabino Canyon and the impressive Arizona-Sonora Desert Museum. The neat thing about Spring Training is that a number of teams have their training sites located in surrounding areas. It certainly wasn't all baseball, but this trip sure centered around it.

On Tuesday, March 22nd, we headed over to the Brewers facility. We hooked up with Freddie and met Tom Skibosh and Mario Ziino, the Brewers Publicity Director and Assistant Publicity Director respectively. Tom left my Mom and I get down on the field; this area was restricted with locked out fencing. I was down by pitcher Don Sutton and he later threw two balls up to me (the first one falling short). I ended up getting on the field again and proceeded to meet Joe Garagiola, Brewers instructor Sam Suplizio, Jim Gantner, Don Money, Gorman Thomas, Mark Brouhard, rookie pitcher Bob

Born on the same day...Gary and Brewers outfielder Charlie Moore meeting at Spring Training.

Gibson (not the famous one) and importantly, Charlie Moore. The club was playing the San Diego Padres on this day and we also met and got pictures of former Brewers star Sixto Lezcano, long-time Dodgers star Steve Garvey, and well-respected Manager Dick Williams (what a super guy). This was incredible stuff for me and I felt like pinching myself. It only gets better because we had the opportunity to meet a gentleman whose name is Dave Fischer. He played baseball with Brewers Manager Harvey Kuenn at the University of Wisconsin-Madison. Dave introduced us to Harvey in his street clothes and I was able to take a picture of Harvey and my Mom just outside of the team's clubhouse. He had brought Harvey a large package of cigars. Padres pitcher Elias Sosa even threw my mother a ball. This was all just very special!

Manager Kuenn on the field looking back to us.

The next day we headed for the stadium at 10:30 and met Freddie coming out of the Brewers clubhouse. I was thankfully able to get inside. The Brewers were playing the Cleveland Indians on this day. I was able to get autographs or at least close pictures of Bert Blyleven, Paul Molitor, Ben Oglivie, Sal Bando, Ned Yost, Larry Haney, former Brave Don

McMahon and Sal's younger brother Chris. I also had the opportunity to talk with both Harvey Kuenn and Don Sutton again. Afterwards, we were driving around Sun City and saw Sal Bando out jogging.

Turning 60 in June of 2013 brought back some nice memories of our trip to Brewers Spring Training 30 years earlier. I knew that Charlie Moore was from Alabama and had been living there after he retired. I would've loved to have him personalize his autograph for me on either or both of the two pictures I'd gotten of us when we had met back in March of 1983. I'd been thinking about it quite a bit and finally decided to pursue it myself on Friday morning, August 9th. I started with a White Pages search of Charlie Moore in Alabama and was not comfortable with what I'd found. By the grace of God, I did a search for Brewers Alumni and found that a Brewers Alumni Association was headed by former major league player, former Brewers coach and current television analyst, Davey Nelson.

An email address was provided there for former Brewers players to contact Davey. I then took the time to write a very sincere email that came from my heart. I asked if I could recruit his help in my efforts to find Charlie Moore and get him to personalize his autograph on the two photos for me. This email was actually sent to Davey at 11:30 a.m. on Friday, August 9th.

After sending it, I walked into our living room. Shortly thereafter, the telephone rang. It was my sister-in-law Shirley confirming what time we were coming up to go out for a fish fry. The call was very short and just after I'd hung up the phone, it rang again. I thought it was her saying she'd forgotten to tell or ask me something. The caller ID said "Milw Brewers." As soon as I answered, I heard Davey's voice. My first comment was "Davey, thanks for calling me!" He said "if only I had contacted him a bit earlier" because he said he was going to be seeing Charlie at a golf outing in Lake Geneva, Wisconsin, that was to take place starting on Monday. I said that I thought Charlie lived in Alabama and he confirmed this was so and that he was to be coming up specifically for this event.

We talked some more in an attempt to solve the dilemma. He said he'd ask Charlie if it would be alright for me to contact him. I said that I would be happy to overnight the photos to the place where he would be staying at while he was there. Davey said that he wouldn't be checking in until Sunday because he had Brewers game responsibilities for both Friday and Saturday night. He

Mom and Brewers Manager Harvey Kuenn outside the clubhouse in 1983.

said if I would clearly put "hold for Dave Nelson" on the package, it should work out okay. Davey then gave me the mailing address for the resort and their telephone number. I thanked him and hurriedly proceeded to get the photos safely packaged and taken over to the post office. I specifically paid for next day delivery and was then asked to fill out labeling paperwork with my return address and the resort's mailing address.

This seemed fine at the time, but after I got home I thought that there may be some problems caused by this new labeling. I had clearly written "please do not bend" and "hold for Davey Nelson" on my original envelope, but the post office attendant transferred this envelope into a larger, white envelope and had only put on the labeling that I'd completed while there. I called the resort and explained what had transpired. They were extremely nice and asked me for the associated tracking number. I was afraid that they'd be confused on Saturday when they read, what had become, an insufficient mailing address. Furthermore, I was concerned that they wouldn't entertain what to do with this envelope until possibly Monday. I then called the post office annex here in town and explained what had happened. The person I talked with was again very nice and she said she'd call over to see if the envelope was still there. I received a call back in about an hour and was told that they had found the envelope and had added the two important comments to its front.

I saw that the envelope was delivered shortly before noon on Saturday. I was then satisfied that I'd done the best that I could to support the timing necessary for the personalized autographs to hopefully take place. On Thursday, August 15th, an envelope arrived to my attention. Its return address was from the Milwaukee Brewers Alumni Association and Nelson was handwritten in this area as well. I was later able to determine that the special golf event in Lake Geneva was called "Swing With The Legends." In the end, timing was everything. Davey had told me that his stop into the office (on the day of my email to him) was intended to be very brief. He could have very easily not even seen my email until some time during the following week. This would have been after this golf outing had taken place and things would have likely gotten a lot more complicated. The courtesy and consideration shown to me by both Davey Nelson and Charlie Moore in this matter is classy stuff and it's very much appreciated.

This story reinforces the most primary lesson associated with this book. God presents numerous opportunities for us to take advantage of in our lives to help us realize our various hopes and dreams. We can choose to pursue them, ignore them, minimize them, sabotage them or put them on hold depending on our own actions or inactions. In this case I had chosen to ignore them, but actually put them on hold for just over thirty years. Completing the equations surrounding our realizations of hope involves the successful meshing of opportunities from God, our associated actions and inactions and the timing of when these variables come together. The opportunities from God are always there in some way, shape or form. Actions were still required on my part in order for the personalized autographs to potentially take place. Thankfully, the timing of my actions enabled the chain of events to take place which resulted in my hope being realized.

The large photo says: "To Gary, Best of Luck, Charlie Moore #22" and the 5x7 photo says: "To Gary, Best Wishes, Charlie Moore #22." I could not be more pleased with the results, regardless of the fact that the determinant actions were first pursued over 30 years later. It's fulfilling to say that everything necessary for this to happen for me took place NOT LONG AFTER TURNING 60.

You Must Answer This

∝ 23 ∾
The EVOLUTION OF LIL GAR

They say what's in a name? I was told that it was my brother who gave me the name Gary. I always felt comfortable with it. The fact that I've been commonly called "Gar" has been more of a compliment in my mind. This has a warm feel to me and I'm more of an informal-type person any way.

My nickname of Lil Gar was actually self-imposed. It first came into being after I'd gotten my accounting degree. It started out as "Poor Lit'l Gar." I enjoyed it because it provided me with sort of a catchy and distinctive identity to have some fun with. Ironically, I'm not that little in stature; being close to five-foot-eleven and over 200 pounds.

The job market was pretty tough during, and even more so, after college. Finding a desirable job, let alone finding an invaluable life partner, were both meritorious challenges. The latter never has had much of anything to do with our business climate, but it's always been arguably the most important and the most formidable of any challenge we may face.

Fortunately, I was offered a nice accounting job prior to graduating. It was the result of an on campus interview and it was for a larger manufacturing company whose headquarters are in Green Bay. I commuted about 50 miles from my mother's home in Neenah for the first seven months that I worked there. It kept my life a bit more scattered until I relocated to within a close walking distance of the office. I had longer hair than the typical accountant, but that isn't saying too much.

I'll never forget one particular Friday afternoon in the small corporate accounting office. There was

Gary as a sailor.

Gary with long hair in college.

one female accounting manager, who was always very nice. She had gotten her hair cut quite short and wasn't real pleased with it. The Controller came out of his office and proceeded to make some sarcastic comments behind me; as he was known to do. He said something like, well, we now only have only one long-haired accountant in the office. When I first got in on Monday morning, I went directly to the Controller's office and asked if I could have five minutes of his time. He said "yes" and I asked him to please invite my boss to join us. My boss was totally awesome, and he knew that I was pretty upset when I left work on Friday. I submitted my two weeks notice. After a couple of more sarcastic remarks from the Controller, he told me that I was free to leave. My boss took this hard, but he respected me for doing it. I was later called at my apartment by the Vice-President of Finance's secretary to arrange a private meeting with him the very next morning in his office. I appreciated it and he asked me to stay in touch.

One of my favorite statements among friends became, "never underestimate Lit'l Gar." I liked challenges and was never much of a follower. When leisure suits came out…I didn't come on board. I was ambitious, but was never a cut-throat or a kiss up. If I couldn't impress people by being the person I was, it didn't appeal to me to change what I stood for in order to do so. Completing my MBA was considered important. I knew public accounting was not for me and I was anxious to prove myself worthy in a manufacturing accounting environment.

You can't be afraid to poke some fun at yourself once in a while either. Lit'l Gar brought out more of a devilish side in me. Yet, my intentions were always innocent and respectful. They never were associated with belittling or harming anyone or anything like that. Over time, the nickname was modified to Lil Gar or sometimes LG. There are many 'Lil Garisms' that have come into existence over the years. Julie will recognize each of these and my friends will recognize many of them.

I don't like getting my picture taken without wearing decent cologne.

Only if they're open (when the place referred to is logically open at the time).

In all sincereiously...

You can't beat food when you're hungry.

I don't like antiques. They're just too old.

Hello and hi... let's do it!

Life is to be lived.

It's just a pretty shade of green.

Here come the garbage goofers!

It could be good or it could be bad, but what if it's not?

Now this is going to a good home.

I like being out there amidst.

Be prepared to smile.

Pre- and post-celebs: include both when you can.

It's time to dance!

I can't believe that you were able to get my name on this.

Fistudily (definition: puttery in a finicky sort of way).

"Waiters" frustrate me (people who typically wait for something to happen TO them).

It's snowbirding out there.

Sometimes you just can't be afraid to sh__ in your pants.

In most things I shoot for 85%; in the important ones I strive for 100 (some things warrant faster decision-making than others).

There are only three ways to go through life and I don't care for the other two choices.

I've always tried to maintain an upbeat personality. With the onset of the muscle disease there are times when I prefer to be more low-key and less engaging than I've been before. I'm most effective when I'm energized and least effective when I overanalyze things. I enjoyed being involved in networking groups and even started one here in town. In my past, it seemed I was most commonly destined to fill some type of leadership role in the groups or organizations I participated in. I took this as a compliment and my tendency was to embrace such capacities. I've reached a stage in my life

Dad and Doug by the bathroom window where Dad fainted when hearing Mom went into labor.

where I'm no longer interested in typical leadership roles. This doesn't mean I've burned out on life, but rather that I now prefer to more subtlely make my presence felt. I've been fully energized by what I believe is a God-driven, passionate desire to write this book.

One of my primary philosophies has always been to not expect others to do something that I would not do myself. Credibility is worth a ton; rather, it's worth at least 53 tons. Authority is given, but meaningful respect is earned. I was raised in a blue collar family. My parents taught me to say "please" and "thank you" and to both open and hold doors for others. This kind of stuff has been second nature to me for a very long time. It's because it's important to me and fundamental to who I am.

I'm a huge principles person. This may bring on some stubbornness, but I will defend what I believe in. I presume other people appreciate it when they can anticipate where you'll stand on an issue or circumstance. Our political system is so disturbing today because here we have a group of intelligent people representing us who are so polarized and fragmented by their association with a specific party, that important issues are simply not being prudently resolved. It seems that their constituents are basically political interest groups. We all have to be willing to compromise our positions when circumstances and conditions warrant. Being consciously in limbo is not a good place to be for very long.

One of the most fundamental convictions in my life is the term 'sense of urgency.' I first learned this term from a divisional General Manager I came to know and respect. He was exceptional and also the very best top management individual that I ever worked with. His name is Dick Parker. I believe the foundation for having a sense of urgency involves consciously conveying a courtesy to others. We do not live in this world alone. We regularly interact with other people. There should be some expectations associated with our behavior. In this case, a reasonable expectation is that others deserve the courtesy of our respect and appreciation for the value of their time.

Being disabled has given me the time and opportunity to take a deeper look into myself. I'm learning to adapt the way I do different things so that I stay compatible with my limitations. Many of these things I used to take

The infamous 'Neenah boys' in 1984; from l to r: Randy W., Gary W., Paul, myself, Randy B., Tim, and Bob.

for granted; I do not anymore. God continues to provide me with numerous blessings. I've consciously learned to have an attitude of gratitude. I've changed over the years, like we all do. I've slowed my pace, expanded my appreciation of little things and most importantly, have deepened my faith. The EVOLUTION OF LIL GAR is continual. I still have much to do here. It likely involves encouraging others to both enjoy and appreciate their lives more, as well as the lives of others around them.

You Must Answer This

ༀ 24 ༁
"We're GOING TO MISS YOU"

I was excited to start my new job as Director of Cost Accounting at Miles Kimball on Monday, February 21, 1994. Up until this point in my career, I had always worked for companies that were manufacturing-based. The associated products would be best described as being extremely diverse. I'd worked with cheese, crushing and screening equipment, ignition parts and accessories, athletic apparel and wood doors.

This company is a direct mail merchandiser of gift items. The position I was hired for was newly created. About 30 percent of their products were manufactured or else involved the need for some type of value-added activity to be done with them.

By the grace of God, I was thankfully able to secure this attractive management accounting position less than two months after the severance pay had expired from my previous job. The company I last worked for was only four blocks away. A place that some of us used to walk to for lunch was about equidistant to both places. I felt extremely fortunate to have found this great opportunity in town, let alone the fact that it was so close to where I'd been working for nearly the last 10 years. My drive to work was basically the same route and it took me about the same amount of time. This just seemed too good to be true, but it was true alright.

I'd left the prior company in quite the unusual manner. On a Friday in late October of 1993, I was given the option of either temporarily staying on and helping out as the company was being actively put up for sale or accepting the immediate termination of my position, with severance. They'd asked for my decision by the following Monday. I was not comfortable becoming a pseudo-employee while giving the appearance to others that everything was business as usual. Julie and I came to the same conclusion after considering the two options. Right away, on Monday morning I told them I chose to accept my immediate termination. I was given severance through the end of the year.

In the course of my second interview with Miles Kimball, I remember the President saying to me, "what's going on over there?"; with regard to the recent happenings at my previous company. Word had gotten out in the community that Morgan Products was undergoing some changes as other positions had been eliminated as well. Things had gotten increasingly stressful there over the last couple of years. It had changed from an awesome place to work to a less enjoyable place to work. The Oshkosh plant, which was by far their largest one, had continued to perform well, but a strained economy was causing profit margins to steadily decrease.

It definitely took me awhile to adapt to the environment at Miles Kimball. It came across as much more laid back and people-conscious than Morgan's had become. I'm not trying to infer that people weren't taking their jobs seriously, but the atmosphere was far less strained than what I'd become accustomed to. They even had specifically defined 'summer hours' during the summer months. Anyone who's familiar with Wisconsin knows that our summers are commonly great times to do things with family and friends. Getting out two hours earlier on Fridays meant the ability to get a jump start on doing something enjoyable like heading up north while beating some traffic, getting in a round of golf or starting an outdoor cook out a bit ahead of time. Full-time employees, with appropriate restrictions, received pay for these attractive 'summer hours' as well.

People seemed to reciprocate the conscious recognition by the company of the validity of such

Gary at Miles Kimball summer party doing some karaoke.

hours. This is a highly seasonal business and things are typically much slower during the summertime. Things change pretty dramatically in the fall. It wasn't uncommon for salaried and hourly employees, who were in less affected areas, to help out the fulfillment and higher stressed areas during the so-called "rush" period. The dynamics seemed to work pretty well. People took pride in their company and wanted to see it continue to do well. It was the classic case of one hand washing the other.

I always liked organizing company bus trips to Brewers baseball games in Milwaukee. I had done so at previous companies and co-workers responded very well to this. One spends a lot of time at work and it was always nice to share some fun times with them and their families. Periodic company parties and larger-scale cook outs were also well received and attended. I enjoyed the opportunity I had to play Santa Claus for a couple of years at the company's children's Christmas party. Space inside of a local theatre complex made for a nice setting. Miles Kimball long had the reputation for having a supportive and healthy work environment. I was again blessed to be involved with a nice group of people. We got along pretty well and friendships were being developed. I had a very intelligent boss who was the company's CFO. He was from Canada and we had a good relationship. By nature, he was definitely much more introverted than I was, but this didn't seem to be causing me any problems. He seemed quite supportive and encouraging of what I was trying to accomplish in my particular role.

I've always believed in the philosophy of trying to work smarter, rather than just harder. In previous companies I gained a reputation for utilizing available MIS-type resources as much as possible. Whenever you can possibly interface comparable data for different purposes, you need to look into it. I selected and implemented a PC-based cost system for help with the capturing and measuring of all value-added activity in the company. Monthly operating statistics and benchmark reports were created to provide effective trend analysis.

In 1997, my responsibilities were broadened when I was promoted to the position of Director of Management Accounting and Treasury. There became a much greater emphasis on cash management than there had been before. My objective was to create a reliable system for daily cash flow recognition and requirements forecasting. I also refined a variable cost per order model for strategic planning purposes. Operations accounting was fun for me because it was dynamic.

I was promoted to the position of Corporate Controller in 1999. There were four managers under my direct supervision and as high a total of support staff as thirteen. It was a good group. One morning in the spring of 1999, the company President stopped in my office and closed the door behind him. He said he wanted to discuss something with me. He knew I came from a strong manufacturing accounting background and he said he wanted to tap into it a little bit. It was clear that he was interested in establishing a means for both measuring and rewarding achievement within the hourly work force. What he was envisioning was an incentive-based system to be designed and developed to encourage improved performance. He wanted it to be a win/win situation whereby the highest achievers would be appropriately rewarded with increased take home pay.

After giving this considerable thought, I came up with something I called the AIM program. The acronym stood for 'activating incentive measures.' To get this accomplished required the considerable help of our Engineering Department. I'd previously worked extensively with product routings and bills of material. In this case we needed to define specific, measurable steps associated with all value-added, as well as some non-value added, activity which the President wanted to become incentive driven. In effect, detail work-center routings needed to be defined by Engineering with a buy-in from the work center supervisors. Plant engineer Jean and Director of Engineering Brent provided the direct support that was needed. The effort to get this accomplished was not only tedious, it was also enormous. The timeframe for getting this implemented was no later than the subsequent 'rush' period, which started in September. We also needed extensive help from Dan, a programmer in MIS, to enable us to capture the necessary data just once for cost, regular hourly payroll and incentive recognition purposes. Numerous, but comparable, work-center graphs were designed and produced. They needed to be able to be run on a weekly basis as well as for a multiple weeks basis.

Our Cost Department and myself worked closely with Engineering and MIS and we made the deadline. There were nearly a hundred different steps or processes that were being captured and given incentive-based consideration during the 'rush' period. We were successfully using the data which was being captured to feed the AIM program, the MACOLA cost system and PEPES. The latter was an acronym given to our regular, weekly payroll system which Dan had wrote in conjunction with my input and stood for 'payroll entry and performance evaluation system.' There was a lot being accomplished and it was as efficient as possible at the time.

During a company Christmas party at the end of 1999, I was recognized as "team member of the year." I know the intentions were good and I was appreciative of this, but I had difficulty saying much in the front

Gary's Team Member of the Year photo art.

of the group. Julie basically needed to speak on my behalf. When it comes down to it, I'm normally a pretty sensitive person with stuff like this. I received a nice personalized 'thumbs up' plaque and a large, colored picture of myself that was produced in our own personalization department. My picture was displayed in a company hallway along with prior 'team member of the year' designees. I never felt comfortable bringing the plaque into my office at work. I'm normally a big believer in recognition when recognition is due, but I hadn't done something like curing cancer or saving someone's life and I recognized that many other people were directly involved with making the incentive-based system happen and work.

Gary's award for 1999.

Gary playing Santa Claus at the children's Christmas party.

By the summer of 2001, when we were purchased by investment bankers, it had become obvious that times for us were strained. The concept of 'summer hours' was long gone. My good friend Bob had retired a year earlier. He, Steve (the Vice President of Inventory Planning and Control) and myself had been going out to lunch together nearly every day for quite some time. We all worked for the same boss and were his direct reports. He would commonly join us. It was good to get away from the office and we all got along pretty well.

Over time, we had been increasingly challenged with defining our specific goals for each year. Direct reporting managers and supervisors were expected to identify their own goals and they needed to be compatible with those of their department heads. Annual performance reviews were the norm, but there was increasing pressure to incorporate progress reviews as well. Then the unthinkable happened. I had completed the reviews for each of my direct reports, got them approved by my boss and made appointments to go over them with each of my people. They each signed off on them and we were moving forward. My boss said he had completed mine as well, but before he talked with me about it, his boss, who was the President gave him his annual review. It was supposedly a brutal one and clearly had caught him off guard. The same was also supposedly true for the reviews given to each of his direct reports. My boss told me he needed to redo my review and that I needed to do the same for each of my managers. Whoa…I'd never experienced something like this before. What do they say… 'wonders never cease.' He told me that I needed to re-think each of their reviews and that I needed to consciously lower my evaluations for each of them.

When he gave me my review, I was devastated. I'd never gotten such a review in my life. It was especially bothersome in that a lot of extremely difficult stuff was successfully worked through with our vendors in the prior year. I felt kind of like a dish rag. It seemed clear that he was following a directive from his boss to humble each of us. If this was the intention, it worked. It sure wasn't motivational. I'd never been placed in such a position in my working years. Then Steve was terminated on August 18, 2001. This was a hard one because I had a great deal of respect for Steve and he was a very conscientious worker.

There was another day that the President stopped in my office to talk and closed the door. In the course of our discussion he looked at me and said, "Gary, I've never fired anyone. They've fired themselves." I was stunned by this comment and did not know how to react to it. At this point a number of salaried people had already lost their jobs there. A number of which had been there quite awhile, including some previous 'team members of the year'.

By the fall of 2002, it was very evident that times had gotten even more strained. I remember a conversation with my boss in my office where he said that people need to realize that what they did for this company yesterday was no longer enough; it's what they can and will do going forward. Not a long time after this, it was becoming apparent that my boss was consciously distancing himself from me. There came a time when he walked partially into my office and said that he wouldn't be going out to lunch for awhile. He gave no reason and I didn't ask for one. In staff meetings I started to feel like I was on an island. He would noticeably attempt to encourage the input of my direct reports and regularly pass over me like I was a guest in the meeting. The worst episode happened in my office one early morning in front of my staff. He basically read me the riot act regarding our lack of focus on goals. I was pretty overtaken by it. Later, each of the people who worked for me came in separately and told me that he was the one who should be ashamed of his behavior.

The die had been cast. I remember coming home that day and telling Julie that something was likely about to happen soon. There was no way I would have been able to continue working very much longer in that environment. Approximately forty percent of the salaried workforce had already been eliminated by then. The remaining members were feeling like they were on a ghost ship.

It was exactly one week before Christmas 2002 and I was called to come to my boss' office. It was my termination day at Miles Kimball. When I walked inside, I found my boss and the Director of Human Resources sitting in a chair to the left of where I was to sit. I was told that my position had been eliminated. I was thanked and told by both of them that I would be missed, but that the company was being actively placed for sale by the investment banking company. The only two words that I said during this one-sided meeting were 'thank you' and this was said only once.

The outplacement contact I was taken downstairs to meet with was surprised by my reaction and readily apparent level of relief. Things had become pretty difficult there and a former co-worker/friend of mine said this normally less than attractive incident probably saved my life. The words "WE'RE GOING TO MISS YOU" have never rang so hollow to me. Thankfully, most of my memories from this company are excellent ones. It was a great place to work for a long time and it can be again.

๛ 25 ๑
Gary, Are You Potentially Open To...

...interviewing for a financial position at a different company? This question came from a former co-worker of mine, whose first name is Reid, when he called me at work in November of 2002. He said that he'd always thought very highly of me and that his boss, the company's President, was to soon begin interviewing to fill a Controller position that would be reporting directly to him.

Fueled by a change of ownership in the summer of 2001, the environment had gotten progressively more stressful where I worked. Some major restructuring had resulted in a considerable reduction and consolidation of both the salaried and hourly work forces. The focus on tightening up the ship was both pervasive and relentless.

I've always been a "people person." The ongoing pattern I'd experienced of seeing co-workers lose their jobs had taken its toll on me. A good number of these people had become friends of mine and I commonly internalized many of their respective losses; and it wasn't just because this frequently involved more work for myself, my staff, or others around me. The last three companies I'd worked for had developed this disturbing trend. This type of environment caused some co-workers to become more protective of their respective job knowledge, more territorial in their work relationships and less trusting of the guise of empowerment.

I'd been through too many formal, comparative staff priority rankings. I wasn't naive enough to think that I was ever immune to this process myself. There were times when I was given a list of rankings to give my opinion on. I was amazed at how little the people who'd made these rankings knew about the efforts of the people involved. Thankfully, I was able to make my case and get some alterations agreed to before mistakes were to be made. At other times, I was at least respectfully asked to initiate such a list involving my subordinates. There should have always been two fundamental questions which were asked in such matters. First, do we need each of the positions that are involved in this determination? Second, are all of the people being ranked satisfactorily performing their jobs? It also seemed that a certain minimum dollar amount of reduction was usually involved with the determination. When "yes" was the answer to the two primary questions, this matter got more complicated. The biggest bang for the buck obviously came from the elimination of the highest paid positions.

I always took pride in being a responsible professional. However, it needs to be a two-way street. Companies were paying me to do a competent job and I expected appropriate consideration from them in return. Being an accounting manager in a manufacturing environment involved being as objective as possible in the carrying out of your duties. I needed to accurately interpret different things for what they were, as well as effectively communicate what I thought they should be.

Performance measurement is one thing. Appropriately identifying the causes and reasons for specific performance is something else. Over the years I worked with a lot of good people. There were well-meaning team players, talented contributors and many who were just a pleasure to be around. I remember thinking at different times, that if I ever had my own company, I would most certainly approach certain individuals regarding their potential interest in coming on board. There were a few people I'd worked with who were exceptionally good with shop floor dynamics. Others were excellent communicators. Some possessed the often underestimated talents associated with "consistently getting things done through people", which remains the textbook definition of a good manager.

I've consciously taken some good and have tried to avoid most of the bad from the people I've had the opportunity to work for. One of my bosses typically took the approach that personnel-type matters would take care of themselves: wrong! I once was in the middle of a very difficult and awkward situation. I was an accounting supervisor at the time and was without hiring and firing authority. My boss hired two sisters to work in the department. One was his right hand person and was there when I started. She worked indirectly for me. Talk about an outstanding worker. She was sharp, conscientious, dependable and definitely not a busy body. Around a year or so after I began working there, he hired her younger sister. I was responsible for eight to ten people during my time with this company. Her sister was also a nice person, but would miss work incessantly. My boss was uncomfortable addressing this issue. A time came when I needed to address it with her. I did so in a private setting; well outside of our department. She seemed to understand, but the fallout I received later from her sister hurt me considerably. You can't just let things, which need to be addressed, continue to simmer and stir. Good supervisors will take into consideration the impact people's behavioral traits have on others and will address matters which deserve addressing. Ironically, I ran into the younger sister a number of years later when she was working at a different job here in town. I was told by another person who worked there that she told him that I was the best boss she'd ever had.

I believe I was a good supervisor and enjoyed helping people develop in their respective roles. I always tried to live by my Dad's philosophy of treating others in a way that I'd like to be treated. It is important for a work environment to be encouraging rather than discouraging. In order to get the most out of people, they need to feel comfortable contributing. You don't talk down to people and you don't think you're beyond reproach. We're all accountable to others in our lives and we're certainly accountable to both God and ourselves. If you can't look at yourself in the mirror, how in the heck can you expect others to meaningfully respect you. I've been faced with doing some very difficult things in work environments, a number of which I did not agree with, but I've always been able to respectfully look at myself in a mirror.

Reid's company was considerably smaller than where I was working, but I appreciated his thoughtfulness and was flattered by his consideration. It definitely sounded worth pursuing further. I promptly mailed him a copy of my resume. A late afternoon interview was scheduled for early December. During this interview my radar came up and I detected some warning signs. I was told upfront that the hiring process associated with this position was expected to be very slow. The President was noticeably inexperienced and Reid's company was also owned by investment bankers. There were to be a series of steps involved before a decision was made.

In the meantime, my present position was eliminated and I was out of work. I was called for a second interview and accepted it. During it, a comment was made by the company President which stuck in my craw. He basically told me not to take it the wrong way, but that I just didn't come across as the typical accountant. He said if he'd have met me outside of the interview process, he wouldn't have believed that I was one. His tone was actually bothersome and he'd told me that his wife worked as a corporate tax accounting manager. The nature of her work responsibilities and associated interactions were considerably different than that of a typical manufacturing accounting manager.

I was later told that I was one of two finalists. A short time after this I received a morning call from the President. I'd already told him that my position had been eliminated. He offered me the job and I respectfully told him that I needed to discuss this with my wife that evening. I said I appreciated it and would call him back early the next morning. A major lesson here is you have to be true to yourself. Even though I'd recently lost a good income and was out of work, the decision was pretty clear. I was uncomfortable with the person I'd be working for and did not believe that this was a good enough fit. Julie strongly supported me as well. I called him the next morning and turned the job offer down.

Reid later called me and told me that his boss told him about my decision. He said he also told him that he thought he may have offended me. I told Reid there were some other issues that concerned me about the position, but that he definitely had offended me. Fortunately, I was streetwise enough to both approach and consider such matters quite objectively. It's usually a mistake to try to rationalize disturbing issues or choose to view them through rose colored glasses. I've always been pleased with this decision. There's absolutely nothing wrong with being POTENTIALLY OPEN TO a job change or a career modification. Just remember…the final decision must be compatible with you and your family. Being compatible always should involve an analysis which takes into consideration much more than just dollars and cents.

❧ 26 ☙
September 1998 – SOSA, McGWIRE and The BREWERS

My favorite play in baseball is the triple. It's fun watching a base runner, whose likely hit a ball somewhere in an outfield gap or it's ricocheting in a corner from one of the foul lines, try to get to third base before he can be thrown out. However, there's nothing like watching the proverbial home run hitter in major league baseball do his thing. We boo when they're intentionally walked and we cheer as we watch the ball travel into the seats.

I've been blessed with being able to grow up watching the great Henry Aaron playing baseball with the Milwaukee Braves; and at the end of his career with the Milwaukee Brewers. During just a twelve day time period in September of 1998, I was able to experience some of the most exhilarating baseball memories that I could have ever imagined.

I always loved playing baseball. Catching fly balls and throwing out base runners were my favorite things to do. Watching someone, I'd just thrown out, turn around and give me a glaring stare was the best compliment I could receive. I enjoyed decoying runners into attempting to take the extra base on balls hit to me in the outfield. Before games and in practices, I looked forward to throwing the baseball to the respective bases. I had an outfielder's arm and took a lot of pride in it.

Over the years I played a lot of baseball. We even had late Wednesday afternoon beer ball games during the summer. There was some good baseball played there. I worked at Medalist Sand-Knit at the time and ordered some attractive, major league style baseball shirts to be custom designed and produced for us. They had their unique numbers with names on the back. Whoever wanted one paid "the price of honor."

I commonly made the mistake of not warming up sufficiently before starting to make purposeful throws from the outfield. My first job out of college was in Green Bay, and I played in two different leagues. One was for

Gary at bat at the age 10.

a very serious team that played using an over-sized softball and the other team was in a more traditional recreation league. I didn't properly adapt my throwing style to the use of a "melon ball", as I called it. There were times after I'd make a throw that I'd experience a burning-type pain in the arm. I never told anyone and would just hope that the next ball was not hit to me, so I didn't need to make an important throw. At the time, my work responsibilities were getting more demanding as well. I played centerfield for the melon ball team and made the decision to leave them after their first ten games. I frequently saw spikes coming in high at second base and the steady level of intensity in this league took the fun out of playing. We won a lot, but my priorities had clearly changed.

As much as I loved Aaron, the best outfielder I ever saw play was Roberto Clemente. I vividly remember attending a Braves/Pirates game with my little league team; our seats were in the lower right field bleachers and Clemente dazzled us with his hustle, defense and world-class throwing arm. My Dad had taken me to numerous Braves games as a young child and this left an indelible mark with me. To this day, baseball is my favorite sport and I've become a die-hard Brewers fan since they moved to Wisconsin in 1970.

On November 6, 1997, the Milwaukee Brewers franchise made the decision to move to the National League for 1998. They were playing in the American League since becoming an expansion team in Seattle in 1969. The Braves were already in the National League when they moved to Milwaukee from Boston in 1953. They stayed in Milwaukee through the 1965 season. I was devastated when they left. I was twelve years old and thoroughly into baseball. How dare they leave us without a team!

Thankfully, the Chicago White Sox and Minnesota Twins were gracious enough to play a few games in Milwaukee until the Brewers arrived. I remember having a fish lunch with my mother at a small, local restaurant in Neenah with my little brown transistor radio sitting on the table top listening to their first home opener in Milwaukee (I still have that radio, by the way). As a kid, that radio was usually glued to my ear somewhere when one of the Braves games was going on. The Brewers had stars like Danny Walton and Tommy Harper.

I'm not as much of a traditionalist as one would think. I loved it when interleague baseball finally came about in 1997. I like National League baseball but I also like the designated hitter feature used by the American League. It's extended the playing career of many good hitters. The fact that major league games are played without a time clock gives them the dignity they deserve. It is so nice to be able to just sit back and let a game simply unfold for you. When you think you've seen everything, something occurs which catches you totally off guard.

The epic home run chase between Mark McGwire of the St. Louis Cardinals and Sammy Sosa of the Chicago Cubs in 1998 was good for major league baseball and its fans. The last player to hit over sixty home runs in a season was the Yankees' Roger Maris in 1961. Ironically, this was the Yankees 61st season of their existence. The great Babe Ruth had previously been the only player to hit sixty home runs in a single season and had done so in 1927. Maris hit number 61 on October 1st–the very last day of the season. His teammate, the great Mickey Mantle, also hit 54 that year.

Like many other baseball fans I got caught up in the excitement of the home run battle between McGwire and Sosa. Myself and a couple of co-workers who regularly went to lunch together were pretty into it by the beginning of September of 1998. One of them, Steve Vestal and I talked about getting to one of the Brewers/Cubs games that was coming up at Wrigley Field in Chicago. One of his wife's best friends lived there and had invited he and his wife to come and stay overnight. When they broached the subject with her that Julie and I would be joining them to attend a game there soon, she invited us all to stay at her place.

Steve drove us to Chicago on Friday, and we saw the Brewers play the Cubs on Saturday afternoon, September 12th. Sammy Sosa hit his landmark 60th home run of the year in this game. The Cubs won 15-12. The Brewers were leading 12-10 going into the bottom of the 9th inning. There were a total of nine home runs in this slugfest. Sosa hit his homer in the bottom of the 7th. They called it one of the Cubs most memorable games of this entire season.

The Brewers' Sept. '98 actual game ticket stubs and program.

Then on Sunday afternoon, September 20th, Julie and I attended the Brewers/Cardinals game at County Stadium in Milwaukee. The Cardinals won it 11-6. Mark McGwire hit his 65th home run of the season as he went 3 for 4 including a double. The Cards blasted five home runs in this game to the Brewers none, but they were outhit 13-10.

Why not save the best for last. I was invited to attend the Wednesday, September 23rd Brewers/Cubs afternoon game at County Stadium by Jeff Janza of Firstar Bank. In my position at Miles Kimball Company, I had worked with and gotten to know Jeff very well. Sammy Sosa was to hit home run numbers 64 and 65 to tie Mark McGwire at the time for the National League home run lead. Talk about exciting...with so few games left in the season. The Brewers won the game in dramatic fashion by the score of 8-7. The Cubs were leading 7-0 going into the bottom of the 7th inning, the Brewers scored four runs in the 7th, one more in the 8th and three unearned runs in the bottom of the 9th for a highly unlikely come from behind win.

Mark McGwire ended up with 70 home runs, and Sammy Sosa finished with 66. Being able to attend these three outstanding games during such a very short time span will always be a special memory of mine. The games involved some historic home runs that were hit by two players who truly gave baseball fans some harmless fascination and a welcome diversion from their everyday lives. The issue of performance enhancing drugs notwithstanding, this was a unique sideshow for major league baseball in a time where they were consciously trying to re-solidify the interest in the sport from their fans. I do not believe either of these players should be elected to the Hall of Fame, but regardless of this belief...the captivating home run battle in SEPTEMBER OF 1998 involving SOSA, McGWIRE and the BREWERS will always bring a smile to my face.

ଓଃ 27 ଞ
AIR PURIFIERS...
WHAT'S AN AIR PURIFIER?

It was the spring of 2003. I had done a lot of soul searching regarding what I wanted to do the rest of my working life. I didn't have any specific answers, but I knew that I had burned out on the world of corporate accounting. At the age of 49 (and soon to be 50), it was clear to me that I needed to find something that: first, I would enjoy doing and second, that I could either earn or provide a decent income from. I found myself being open to more options than I'd ever been in my past.

I received an email in April which referenced a business opportunity that kind of intrigued me. I decided to formally respond to it and completed the requested information. This was pretty unusual for me because I normally was quite cautious about this kind of stuff.

Julie had gotten very concerned about me in the previous couple of years. This was a direct result of a combination of two unrelenting and pervasive things in my life. There was the seemingly ever-increasing stress level associated with my job. Next, there were my proactive attempts to successfully overcome the considerable complications that were associated with my mother's advanced age and her worsening health issues.

I was diagnosed with Graves Disease in the fall of 2001. My office was on the third floor and I would commonly be up and down the flights of stairs a number of times during the typical day. It got to a point where I would find myself significantly out of wind when I would climb back to the second and third floors. I'd find my heart beat racing when I'd get up from my desk to write on my white board, my legs would shake, and I'd lost a noticeable amount of weight without trying to do so. Some co-workers were expressing their concern, and I remember one person telling me, "please don't lose any more weight Gary."

I wasn't oblivious to what was going on in my life in this regard. I just didn't know what to do about it. I was making a very good income and cared the world for my wonderful Mom. She'd always been there for me and I wasn't about to let her down when she needed me the most. Near the end of 2002, my bucket was overflowing. Julie had given me her permission and encouragement to resign from my Controller position. I found this to be easier said than done. I never was a quitter, did not typically back off from challenges and saw myself as the primary breadwinner in our family. Does this sound familiar to anyone? I was actually done a huge favor on December 18th when I was called in to my boss's office and told that the company was being put up for sale and that my position had been eliminated.

I had been thinking more seriously about considering other income alternatives while still working there. Franchise ownership was one of the things I was looking into. I arranged a meeting with a regional manager of Minuteman Press. We met at one of their existing locations in Appleton. He provided me with a nice tour, described their typical operation and explained their business model. The concept of royalty payments and performance-based commissions came into play. I also met with a local business owner who I learned was interested in selling his business. I envisioned this opportunity as one which would be most attractive as a shared partnership with another owner. I approached another individual that I'd worked with who had what I believed was a compatible background. It was just too risky and we both moved on.

I've learned from years of experience that one's health needs to always come first. Good health is really made up of a number of things. Many of these things are obvious and many of them are not. The importance of a person's mental well-being is often underestimated. We're always concerned with avoiding outcomes such as: strokes, nervous breakdowns and heart attacks. Ulcer prevention and addressing a person's mental well-being are much lower on the typical list of concerns. How about unobvious depression? The urgency factor for addressing each of these latter, health-related, factors is commonly much lower.

Thankfully, another major Godincidence occurred when I was contacted on the telephone in early April of 2003 by Dave Ingram from Baytown, Texas. He had an extensive corporate information systems background and I was very impressed by what he had to say. Being a numbers guy, I usually do not get easily fooled by or over-zealous with regard to references to various opportunities to generate huge income streams. Thankfully, Dave was not that kind of person or I would have been turned off early on. However, this did not, by any means, minimize the need to examine the associated numbers and the respective business model. The company's name was EcoQuest International, and they were recognized as the world leader in air purification technology. The opportunity involved was to become a "virtual franchise" of the company which was headquartered in Greenville, Tennessee.

Julie and I talked about this extensively, and we decided to take the next step and try out one of the filter less "whole home" air purification units on a one week, no obligation basis in our home. We saw this short-term trial as featuring nothing to lose with hopefully, something very worthwhile to gain from it. If anyone would have told me that we'd have a business, out of our home, selling air purifiers I never would have believed them. I'd previously never sold anything repetitively in my life. My only meaningful prior sales claim was of a used Camaro on carsoup.com. However, we came to believe that the combination of associated products and the residual income aspect of this attractive direct marketing business was worthy of our attention and pursuit.

We established an S Corporation at the beginning of May. We also came out of the blocks on fire. In our first 90 days we earned the noteworthy rank of Sales Manager. I recognized the importance involved with attaining this rank as soon as possible. This was the minimum timeframe required for earning, what I viewed as, this game-changing position. In our first six months in the business, we qualified for a company bonus car. It was a gorgeous, azure blue Jaguar S-type. This was the shortest possible time period identified for meeting the necessary requirements for earning one of the company's executive bonus cars. Julie helped whenever she could spare some time, but her teaching job has kept her more than busy over the years. She would usually help me on

Friday nights and weekends when we exhibited our products at various trade and home and garden type shows.

The leader of the company was a man named Michael Jackson. He is definitely the most effective motivator and business promoter that I have

Our EcoQuest blue Jaguar S-type bonus car.

ever met or seen. He was able to gain the utmost respect and admiration of people all over the world who got to know him. I've never seen anyone quite like him and probably never will again. We bought in and our efforts were nicely rewarded for a significant period of time.

Over a considerable number of months, we would typically at least hit the minimum defined target to allow us to receive the maximum allowable bonus car payments. Our efforts in the business enabled us to earn two new executive bonus cars and our associated success gave us the opportunity to roll over our first, cherished, bonus car for a second two-year term rather than select a different car. We actually earned the equivalent of three company bonus cars. I developed a sincere passion for this business and actually came to enjoy it a great deal. What was fascinating was the interest I gained in pursuing each of its possible aspects. One of the intriguing things about EcoQuest is that one could focus their attention on an array of different things or one or more very specific things. There was business building, face to face product retailing and participation in trade or home and garden type shows. A commercial aspect was also available and I became certified as an indoor air quality specialist.

We achieved the nice rank of Coordinating Sales Manager in just our third year. This meant that we had at least three different Sales Manager legs in our business. We enjoyed bringing on numerous respected partners and met many interesting and wonderful people along the way. Thankfully, we've been able to develop lasting friendships with a number of these people. Our attendance at the annual conventions held in different cities and for various events and purposes was something we regularly looked forward to. We finished in the TOP 25 in product retailing for four consecutive years, including achieving as high as 9th place in 2006.

9th in EcoQuest International for Retailing Excellence in 2006.

As always, with Julie's help, we earned our first ever cruise to New Brunswick and Nova Scotia. This also got us back to Manhattan, as it left from New York Harbor. Ironically, I was able to incorporate seeing my first and only game at the old Yankee Stadium in its final year versus their most hated rival, the Boston Red Sox in August of 2008.

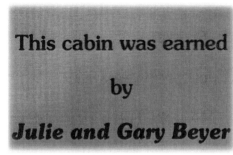

This cabin was earned by Julie and Gary Beyer

This plaque was on our door for the cruise.

The last couple of years of our involvement with the business were very difficult. It seemed that the company was experiencing major infrastructure issues. In hindsight, I believe they were spreading themselves too thin. They had branched out into energy management and this got my attention, as well as the attention of other business owners like ourselves.

At the time, I was involved as President of a local business networking group which I had gotten started in our area. I asked if anyone could recommend an electrician for me to talk with who might be interested in some type of partnership with me in this regard. One of the members said he'd talk with his electrician friend, Greg, about it and it ended up that the two of us hit it off. The intention was for us to establish appointments to introduce the product offerings to prospective customers, most of which were small to medium-sized businesses. Our combination of skill sets seemed to work well. He preferred to focus on the larger commercial opportunities. He'd worked on substations and his background was extremely strong in such things as power factor correction issues and line disturbances.

There needed to be a commitment of resources to acquire some of the expensive commercial products. Greg wasn't able to

Recognition on stage by company President Mike Jackson.

split any of these costs with us at the time. Julie and I talked it over, and she reluctantly agreed for us to invest a little over $13,000 in a handful of specific products which he thought were the most appropriate. We were able to pursue some appointments, and the actual presentations were very well received. Greg was the technical expert and product installer. I trusted him implicitly. He purchased some electrical monitoring software and portable power factor detection equipment. We would get together regularly and discuss our plans of attack. All of the products were serialized, and he'd regularly keep some of this product in his truck.

On Sunday morning, June 21, 2009, I received a call from the member of the networking group who'd facilitated Greg and I meeting. He told me that he was tragically killed in a motorcycle accident up north the night before. Greg had told me on Friday afternoon that he was going there to visit a long time friend. I was devastated. It was also my birthday. This brought a dramatic close to the energy management part of our business. One of the products that Greg had taken in his truck a few weeks prior has never been found. It was worth just under $2,000. The other product equipment he had of ours was found in a storage shed that he'd been renting. This was broken into only a short while before his tragic death. As I said earlier, I trusted Greg implicitly, and I never had him sign any type of paperwork when he took any of the product equipment that we had purchased. The lawyer for his estate would not give us any recognition or consideration for the cost of this piece of unrecoverable product equipment. Thankfully, I was able to pay a re-stocking fee and return the remaining commercial equipment back to the company.

This pretty much took the wind out of my sails. I had already gotten away from the other aspects of the business because it had become clear that my advancing muscle condition was no longer compatible with working it. We were in this business for a little over seven and a half years. Julie and I will always look back on it favorably. It was such a refreshing, enjoyable and rewarding change from the corporate accounting world I was accustomed to. I never did fit the mold of the traditional accountant. There's another thing for sure, if I ever hear someone say, "AIR PURIFIERS…WHAT'S AN AIR PURIFIER?", I will definitely be able to give them an accurate and complete answer.

ல 28 ஐ
Excuse Me, You've Been Selected
By American Express To Be
TODAY'S FANS OF THE GAME

Good friend and former co-worker Bob Snyder and I had always talked about attending a Green Bay Packers away game some time. Packer football is kind of a religion around here. Many people would sooner miss out on receiving a free five-course meal at one of the area's finest restaurants than miss watching a Packers game. We finally decided to go to Dallas to see the Packers play the Cowboys there on November 14, 1999.

We found out that it was the Cowboys 40th anniversary season. Bob went through Packer Fan Tours and purchased two tickets for us via credit card. They appeared to be nosebleed type seats in one of the corner end zone areas, but so what…at least we'd be at the game.

It's got to be pretty difficult going through one's adult life if their spouse is not a Packers fan; let alone if they're a serious fan of another team. As a child, you don't understand the magnitude of this commitment. However, there's no excuse for underestimating this as an adult. I am being facetious, but anyone who's been to a game at Lambeau Field in Green Bay will see first hand how far some fans will take their loyalties.

Being 60 years old, I remember the glory days of the 60s. Those Packers teams were coached by Vincent T. Lombardi and led by former seventeenth round draft choice, Bart Starr. There were

Bob Snyder with the two American Express reps in Dallas in 1999.

the infamous Packers sweeps run by Paul Hornung and Jim Taylor. As Lombardi used to say, "winning isn't everything, it's the only thing." These teams didn't just win, they won championships.

I'll never forget my Dad taking me over to the Labor Temple hall in Neenah to watch the Packers vs. Cowboys championship game played on December 31, 1967. I was 14 and understood the priorities associated with helping our Packers win this game. It's commonly referred to as "The Ice Bowl"; you may have heard of it. It was 15 below zero at game time, the wind chill was minus 48. The game was available there on closed circuit television. It was otherwise blacked out around our area. Talk about cold! It was cold inside the Labor Temple. There were so many people there you'd swear there were some major giveaways, maybe there were. Fortunately, the Packers won 21-17 to get to the second Super Bowl. They'd previously won the first Super Bowl ever played in January of 1967 after beating Dallas in the preliminary league championship game. If they would have lost, a few less people may have left the hall. There may have been a need for some sacrifices.

There've been some great years and awesome memories associated with Packers football. There also were some very lean years. I remember them too. We were excited about the Gold Dust twins of Donny Anderson and Jim Grabowski, but not that excited about Eddie Lee Ivery and Gerry Ellis. Between 1979 and 1994 the Packers had only five winning seasons. It didn't feel much like Titletown during this time, but we held onto the name nonetheless. After all, whose name is on the Super Bowl trophy?

About a week or so before we were going to leave, a co-worker of ours found out that singer Shania Twain was going to be filming a concert there right after the game. It was going to be shown during Thanksgiving time. We were like…that should be pretty cool to see live too. We landed in Dallas and picked up our rental car. We were going to be staying at a nearby hotel that featured a shuttle service to and from the game. We'd planned to stay a few extra days and see some of the sights both in and around Dallas.

We were Packerized for our stay. The Saturday night before the game, we went out for some Texas BBQ and found Dallas fans to be very friendly. The Cowboys featured three offensive stars in Troy Aikman, Emmitt Smith and Michael Irvin. What was ironic was, they were each hurt and not going to be playing in this game. All we kept hearing is "you guys are going to kill us" or "you sure came at the right time." We proudly wore our green and gold shirts, logo-emblazoned hats and beads.

Leaving early enough the next morning, we wanted to get there in time to watch pre-game workouts, etc. When we arrived inside the stadium lot, it got pretty exciting. We saw the large pictures on the

Picture of field after we'd gotten to our new seats.

stadium sides of current Cowboys stars and a buzz was becoming evident. They gave us a yellow wrist band at the gate to be displayed for the Shania Twain concert. We were getting pretty excited and proceeded to find the ramps we needed to use to get up to our seats. They were definitely in the highest row, but at least we were there. We had a straight-on view of the large, impressive jumbotron screen that was in the opposite end zone corner.

There was hardly anyone seated when a younger guy and gal, carrying a white plastic bag, approached us with this hard to believe proposal. Ironically, we were proudly wearing our Packers gear. The guy said we'd been chosen by American Express to be "today's fans of the game." We both looked at each other and were totally stunned by this comment. This was just too unreal! They said we'd be taken to a couple of awesome seats which were nicely located above the Cowboys bench by the 50-yard line. At this point, it sounded too good to be true. Then the girl opened up the white bag to show us a number of neat, souvenir-like items which were inside. We were to be given this bag that featured Cowboys 40th anniversary surprises. There were a couple t-shirts, a small pennant, a couple of hats and some programs. Then the convincer really came out. The guy was carrying this large, over-sized version of an American Express card. He said all we'd have to do was stand and clearly hold up this sign when the stadium announcer

The oversized American Express card we were given to hold up.

referenced today's fans of the game. The card measures 15 inches wide by 23-3/4 inches long and says Texas Stadium on it.

It turned out that there were four such "fans of the game" seats. Very early on game day, they were directly offered to selective fans inside the stadium who'd been identified as having the worst seats and who'd bought their tickets using American Express. The winners were approached on a first identified, first talked with basis. Thank God we came over early and went up to our seats right away. There were 64,634 people who attended this game. To be presented with this incredible opportunity made the whole experience extremely special for us. Here we were, right in the midst of some very serious Cowboys fans, decked out in our best Packers gear. It left little doubt who we were cheering for.

The game itself was another story. The Cowboys, led by backup quarterback Jason Garrett (who's, ironically, now their head coach) beat the Packers on this day 27-13. To make matters worse, former Packer defensive back George Teague had a back-breaking 95-yard interception return for a touchdown which sealed the deal. So much for the Packers killing the injury riddled Cowboys. Regardless of this outcome...we thoroughly enjoyed ourselves.

After the game, a large stage was set up for the concert. My seat was on an aisle and Bob's was right next to me. We thought; we're going to have an awesome view of this concert too. It was by our side of the field centered around the fifty yard line. It turned out that the performance was to be facing the opposite direction from us. This didn't seem to matter much though as the concert was excellent. What's kind of interesting is that when my wife and I later watched the replay that I'd taped from television, you could frequently spot Bob and myself cheering. We were at the right height and location to be easily seen through the various stage shots.

As we walked back to the shuttle bus after the end of the concert, we said that no one would ever believe our story. Upon taking a seat in the second row behind the driver, we continued to discuss what had happened to us. It seemed like a dream. I heard a guy who was sitting right in front of us, next to a lady, quietly murmur to her…."who are they trying to kid?" What is cool is I still have the very large American Express sign as another means of proof for our 'hard to believe' story. Not too many people will be bestowed with this unique piece of sports memorabilia.

We were thankfully able to take in a tour of the Cowboys stadium before leaving Dallas. I'll never forget walking out to mid-field and experiencing the very noticeable crown which existed on the field's surface. Their facilities were quite impressive. The rivalry between the Packers and Cowboys will remain strong forever. There's just too much history for it to ever lose its steam.

Just never say never. You just do not know when someone may approach you at your next attended sporting event and say, "excuse me, YOU'VE BEEN SELECTED TO BE TODAY'S FAN OF THE GAME." Hopefully, you will also be able to prove it if you later hear someone say, "who is he or she trying to kid?"

You Must Answer This

❧ 29 ❧
THE WISE SAGE

The title for this story was actually recommended to me by my wife Julie. Over the years she has regularly heard me praising former co-worker, and now long-time friend, Bob Snyder for his considerable level of wisdom and depth of character. We've become very close and I have a high regard for him and what he stands for. We both held accounting management positions under the same boss for a number of years. I've found him to be a person of very high integrity who is thoroughly genuine and doesn't sugarcoat things. He also is one who is never quick to make rash judgments.

He can outwardly seem like someone who'd be pretty set in his thoughts, but I've found him to consistently be highly rational, while typically attempting to see both sides of a situation or circumstance. He is refreshingly grounded and I truly enjoy his company.

I started working at Miles Kimball Company in Oshkosh in February 1994. I was hired to fill the new position of Director of Cost Accounting. Bob was the Director of Financial Accounting. He had been there for many years and was already there when new ownership had taken over the company. This change in ownership had brought in a different Chief Financial Officer, who was our boss and was also the same gentleman who hired me.

My prior work environment had turned unbelievably stressful over my last few years there. The work atmosphere here was totally different. It was much more low key and they even had special early out work schedules planned for Fridays during the summer. This included all office staff and it was common for people to leave two hours earlier than normal on Fridays. Talk about refreshing! It took me awhile to adapt to this more people-oriented environment because it was such a change from what I'd been experiencing.

We had separate staffs and our respective responsibilities most commonly crossed paths during the company's regular monthly closing cycles. It was obvious that Bob was well respected by the people there, but he seemed to be more introverted than myself and our friendship took awhile to develop. We both were huge Packers fans; however, many people are here in Wisconsin.

I was feeling very strained by my desire to take responsibility for resolving some important matters regarding my Mother. She was still living in her home and was recovering from two hip replacements. The first was caused by a fall and the second was caused from the deterioration associated with excessive dependence. It was a larger house which needed a lot of work to be done before it could be put up for sale. I always tried to err on the side of maintaining her independence because she'd always been such an independent person. I loved her dearly and it had become obvious that she needed to be moved into a less threatening environment. As time passed, my office was relocated next to Bob's. He'd become a much appreciated sounding board for me.

The Director of Inventory Planning and Control position was placed under our boss. Steve Vestal was in this role and the three of us would regularly go out to lunch together. Steve was from Minnesota, and is a dreaded (but mild mannered) Vikings fan. We each got a long very well and looked forward to our regular lunchtime discussions. Bob and I had talked

Bob Snyder and Steve Vestal at our mini-bowlarama.

about attending a Packers away game at some point in the future and our interest in doing so was becoming more serious.

In the fall of 1999, Bob approached me regarding my level of interest in going to an upcoming Packers game that they were scheduled to play in Dallas on November 14th. I talked with Julie about it and she said...why don't you go? We did and had a great time there. Our friendship was growing because I believe we had developed a good deal of mutual respect for each other. While in Dallas we went to Dealey Plaza and visited the sixth floor museum there. We eerily reflected at the various sites associated with President Kennedy's assassination. We'd rented a car and also drove over to Fort Worth and spent some time in Cow Town. We also visited Billy Bob's very large saloon that is there.

Over the years we've gone to three Packers away games together. We also attended games in Tampa and New York and took advantage of the opportunities to incorporate some sightseeing too. While in Tampa, we were graciously invited to a tailgate party by some avid Buccaneer fans and will never forget their over the top, conspicuously extravagant "Da Bucs" bus. Bob drove over the causeway and we were able to get inside the Tampa Bay (nee Devil) Rays baseball

Gary and Bob in Tampa in 1995.

stadium and visit the first ever Hooters restaurant that is located in Clearwater. In New York City, we spent considerable time at Ground Zero, Madison Square Garden, Time Square and Rockefeller Center (where the extensive Christmas decorations were still there to be appreciated).

Neither of us had ever taken the Packers Tour at Lambeau Field. This was surprising because we were longtime Packers fans. We'd even taken in the Cowboys Stadium Tour when in Dallas, as well as a tour of the Rangers Ballpark in Arlington. One afternoon when the two of us were in Green Bay, we decided to check it out and were surprised when there was no line. We had just bought tickets and a gentleman standing very near to this area heard us telling the story of how we'd been to Dallas, Tampa and New York to see the Packers play but had never been on a Packers tour. This gentleman turned out to be Jerry Parins, the Packers Head of Security. He came over to talk with us, and to make a long story short; he took us on a very special, personalized tour of the facilities. This included an elevator trip down to see the Packers empty locker room area, the position coaches rooms and the impressive stadium security area. At a later date, Jerry directly helped us in our efforts to purchase four tickets for the Giants at Packers game of Sunday, October 3, 2004. We told him more details of our trip to New York in early 2002 (after 9/11) and that we wanted to pay back our friend from New York who'd invited us there for that game by getting him and a friend to see his Giants play at Lambeau.

I've definitely learned to both highly respect and value Bob's considerable depth and wisdom. He's a genuine and compassionate friend in my life. I always treasure and enjoy our regular get togethers and conversations. Bob retired a few years before my position was eliminated at Miles Kimball. He retired in July of 2000 and my position was eliminated on December 18, 2002. We've become very good friends and our friendship has grown through the sharing of challenges in our lives. After I received the troublesome call on that Friday afternoon that I'd been diagnosed with a rare type of incurable muscle disease, he was the first friend that I chose to call because I needed to listen to his wisdom. He most certainly deserves to be referred to as THE WISE SAGE.

❧ 30 ❧
In Recognition Of SOME TRULY SELFLESS BEHAVIOR

My mother was always someone who seemed to get her greatest satisfaction by doing something nice for other people. She didn't do things to get attention or because she received credit for doing them. It meant a lot to her to see someone smile, or watch another person get relief or enhance someone's confidence because she'd helped them in some way.

I saw her commonly put herself second to others in numerous circumstances. Her level of selfless behavior was impressive, if not exemplary. The beneficiaries of her actions, like myself, sure noticed. There were times I took it for granted, as did others, but the key here is she did such things because she wanted to, not because she had to or needed to.

People exhibiting selfless behavior often fail to get any type of recognition. The immediate beneficiaries typically appreciate it, but beyond this their efforts may blend into the woodwork as far as others are concerned. To this day, I try to make it a point to acknowledge people's selfless behavior. Recently, a local Perkins restaurant manager quietly went out of his way to help two ladies get safely outside. One lady was clearly a younger caregiver for the other. Whe Mike came back in the restaurant, I went over to him and said, "that was pretty classy my friend." He said, "Gary, I was just doing my job." It was much more than that and as I got outside, I heard the ladies talking about what he had done. They were clearly impressed. I excused myself for interrupting them, but couldn't help but express further praise for his display

Gary at 21 and his very special Mom.

of consideration. This type of behavior should not be taken for granted, but it commonly is.

When I was in the corporate world I had the opportunity to work closely with many people. I realized that selfless behavior had nothing to do with a person's level of responsibility or education. There were many times when I experienced someone quietly going above and beyond. In a number of these cases, there was little to no recognition of it. They simply were expected to do it; when in reality...it definitely had stood out. I would quietly tell them that I was going to make their supervisor aware of it and would commonly inform this person's boss as well. Thankfully, selfless people are not hampered by the lack of recognition for their actions; I believe if they were, some really cool things would not take place.

My good friend since college, Gary Ludwig, has always been a genuinely kind person. They do not come any nicer or more considerate. When it comes to helping others, he's pretty special. He's taken considerable time to reach out to me in an effort to understand some of the less obvious health-related and personal challenges I've been working through for awhile. I'll never be able to adequately express my level of appreciation to him.

I'd not been to a Packers practice before. In July of 2012, he invited me to join him, his two sons and one of their friends to attend their very first practice of training camp. We had a good time. In early August I played back a voicemail message from Gary. It said, "Gary, I wanted to let you know that I've left a package outside of your front door." His over and above efforts provided me with an unforgettable, Packers-related surprise. I was honestly quite overwhelmed. My wife had gotten home from work and as I opened and went through the box, the tears began to flow. This was honestly one of the most touching moments of my life. What got to me the most was that I understood what his intentions were.

In November of 2012, I was told I needed to have emergency retinal re-attachment surgery in my left eye. The surgery needed to be done in Green Bay the very next day. There was little time to react and with such short notice, I was totally humbled to find Gary waiting in the recovery room with Julie. Then on Tuesday, April 23, 2013, he facilitated our private visitation for the taping of a sports roundtable talk show to be conducted in Appleton. This also gave me the opportunity to finally meet the show's host, Dennis Krause. I'm a big fan of this show and even though we'd never met before, we had developed a kind of 'mutual respect friendship' from our numerous prior email communications. Dennis has quietly shown himself to be extremely classy as well. I'm seldom caught speechless, but Gary's gotten to me a few times in just this last year alone. He represents the best in us all. The many people who've had the pleasure of getting to know him over the years are truly quite fortunate.

After needing similar, next day emergency surgery on my right eye on December 13, 2012. I was given strict instructions to be as low key as possible for awhile. Shoveling or plowing snow was a "no no" and here we are at the start of a Wisconsin winter. Julie has serious back problems so we were in a predicament. Thankfully, we have nice neighbors. Julie called and asked a couple of them for their help. Not only did they willingly offer their help, they handled all of our snow-related issues the entire winter and we had a lot of snow too. This has been a prolonged period of considerable stress for us. I always considered myself as someone who would more than carry his own weight. I tried to be the strong one during my family's health challenges. Over the years, I've been pretty healthy and I willingly accepted the responsibility of trying to be there for them like they had been for me. Now, we needed help and we weren't too proud to ask for it. Our sincerest thanks goes out to Dave and Barb Kersztyn.

I'll never forget being totally caught off guard one day while at work. A former co-worker, Rick Ramirez, knocked on my office door to surprise me with an autographed Ralph Kiner baseball. He and I have since become good friends, but our paths didn't cross that often at work. Like Gary, he meant so well by doing this and it really touched me. My reputation as a huge baseball fan was pretty well known and he knew that I would treasure this. We try to get together once in awhile for either breakfast or lunch and even for a Brewers game or two. It's fun talking sports with him and we have very similar values. He too has overwhelmed me a few different times with his exceptional level of consideration and kind ways. Rick was able to get me inside the TV broadcast booth at Miller Park in Milwaukee for a couple of innings this past year. I've experienced, first-hand, this man's tendency for exhibiting selfless behavior. He is one very classy person.

I'd be remiss if I didn't acknowledge the considerable uninitiated encouragement that I continue to receive from three other Garys in my life. Our dentist, Dr. Gary Dubester, has developed into a wonderful friend and has been a staunch supporter of mine over the last many years. His level of empathy for others runs deep. I can't tell you how many times he checked on me as I was dealing with my eye-related issues. I could hear it in his voice. He's been concerned. He's been considerate and he's been a steady sounding board for me. My long-time friend Gary West has regularly taken considerable time to help keep me upbeat. The man is positive, positive, positive! He lives in Oregon, but that hasn't mattered. He continues to be there for me and, like most of us he has his own challenges. Then there's Gary Madsen. We went to school together as well. He and his wife Linda are people of faith. They've been, and continue to be, directly faced with some very difficult things in their lives. They both stay positive and regularly take time to encourage others. Each of these 'Garys' have displayed considerable efforts to reach out to me. I want them to know that both Julie and I deeply appreciate it.

When you're diagnosed with a supposedly incurable disease, and then this gets compounded with some other unavoidable complications, you realize that your metal is being aptly tested. It causes you to learn a lot more about yourself, but you also learn considerably more about the people around you that you've come to know. I've not been one to deny this type of thing or to attempt to run from it either. I've become much more intrigued by and appreciative of other people's displays of selfless behavior. When you're the actual beneficiary of such class, it touches you all the more. It's not self-serving, it's done without commotion and it's unselfishly considerate.

What a wonderful concept, people who get tremendous satisfaction out of doing nice things for other people. I'm proud to say that Julie and my sister-in-law Shirley satisfy this distinguished criteria as well. I've been the beneficiary of this trait a good many times too. These people may not want or need any attention brought to them for doing so, but, on my behalf, this story is intended

to bring some much deserved recognition for their TRULY SELFLESS BEHAVIOR. Most importantly, their credit has already been given to them. It's through their internal degree of self satisfaction, which was specifically derived from what they've done for others.

Three proven selfless ladies: Shirley, Julie, and my mother.

❧ 31 ☙
STACK 'EM HIGH
and WATCH 'EM FLY

Most people know the stereotype of the typical accountant. They're usually viewed as being more introverted by nature, and categorized as especially 'good with numbers'. When parties are thrown, they're commonly not invited or given the wrong address and time. Being the brunt of jokes for years, they've become accustomed to their stereotyped fate. Businesses look to them for stewardship, but away from them for representation.

I worked in the corporate accounting world for over twenty eight years. Friends and co-workers consistently told me that I didn't come across as the typical accountant. They'd usually be quick to add, but don't take this the wrong way. I normally didn't. I took it as a compliment. You see, I've never seen myself as typical anything.

I didn't have an adversarial mentality as a manufacturing accountant. One of the very nicest compliments I've ever received was from Mike Flanigan, the former Plant Manager at Morgan Products. Mike once said to me, "Gary, you're the best accountant I've ever worked with. You try to work with us, rather than against us. Others seem to always be looking to find something wrong with what we're doing." I learned a long time ago, that meaningful respect is earned and not given. Regardless of what you're doing, it's always better to try to work with people rather against them. As my mother used to say, "you get more with sugar than you do with vinegar."

As the years went on in the corporate environment, I came to feeling more and more like a fish out of water. I always tried to do my job as objectively as possible, but also found myself, many times, seeing a considerable amount of gray. Fundamental accounting principles will commonly ignore or consciously try to eliminate gray, but gray should not be either ignored or eliminated. Gray, in such environments, usually involves recognizing the dynamics associated with people working within the various settings.

People deserve to be treated with respect and dignity. Unlike machines, you don't simply turn them off and on when you desire to. I've seen way too many people lose their jobs over the years. A number of them have not come back that well. Some lose confidence, some stay mired in "the blame game," and some just give up. Others change careers or their life paths. I consciously chose to change my life path.

I knew that I had burned out specifically on the corporate accounting world. Sure, it paid well, but it had taken its toll on me too. My wife Julie will tell anyone who'll listen that she was afraid she was going to lose me in some manner while I was nearing the end of my last corporate job. I've had a tendency to internalize things that have happened in these environments. They didn't just have to happen to me directly either. I was regularly given and knowingly accepted the responsibility of telling people who worked under me that their jobs were being eliminated. I never hid from this responsibility when I was employed, but I ran from it after I decided that this was no longer something that I wanted to be involved with. I understand the need for change and that change often impacts peoples' lives, but as I've said before "blood runs through my veins, not water."

I thought about changing careers; however, it was too late to get into sports broadcasting. I once wanted to do play by play for major league baseball games. I was much younger and unmarried when this regularly passed through my mind. What do they always say…do what you love and the money will follow. I believe that there's a high degree of validity in this point, but it has to be tempered with reality and must fit in with both self-imposed and uncontrollable constraints. I did not have 'the answer' or even an answer. When you're responsibly married, and shaving in the mirror at 49 years old this is quite unsettling. How about when you view yourself as the primary breadwinner in your marriage and your new reality says that you're not.

Thankfully, the grace of God caused me to open my eyes to something outside of my comfort zone. After working in the world of corporate accounting for so many years, this major change of pace business opportunity provided me with a welcome outlet for some previously untapped, unrecognized and unrealized skills. The challenge I drew from it became very exciting for me. The more I looked at it, fortunately openly, the more it seemed to make good sense. Why not me, why not now...why not featuring air purifiers?

I've never been one to do things half way. If I'm going to commit to something, I'm not just going to put my toe in the water for awhile and hope for the best. You can't be sort of pregnant. As I've commonly said, sometimes you can't be afraid to sh__ in your pants. I believed I needed to invest in some product inventory. Julie and I talked about it and she supported my plan. I believe in crawling before you walk and walking before you crawl, but my 'sense of urgency' mentality said, let's facilitate walking sooner...rather than later. Inventory was not purchased to just sit in the shed we had purposely built for our business. It needed to be moved and talked about with others and placed for trial and sold. This mantra was not a once or twice a week goal. It became nearly an everyday goal. I developed a "refuse to lose" mentality. Failure was simply not an option.

It became clear that there were different ways to move product in the business. I loved that about it. People could readily hear the enthusiasm in my voice and detect the energy in my associated actions. Gary was an accountant for goodness sakes. Lil Gar was to become a type of storm trooper. I woke up in the morning ready to get after it. A gentleman, and now good friend that I helped bring into this business, named John Steshetz, told me that the reason he decided to get involved is because he loved the energy and passion that he felt from myself and others that were already involved in it. They weren't happy because they were conned into something. They were happy because they were enjoying what they were doing while also making some very good money at it.

I used to literally fill my car with products. This commonly included every available space. I'd head out for a day with the intention of returning home with an empty or near empty car. In all honesty, there were a number of times when this occurred. I liked the challenge of it and took it seriously. There were many times that I didn't have a specific game plan of making particular stops. I usually had a couple places in mind or at least a direction to head for upon leaving the house, but I consciously did not restrict or pressure myself by being held to a list of stops. I'd commonly choose, what I believed were, 'good times' to approach each type of business. I'd always ask to speak to a decision-maker and never just left my card or product-related materials. If I couldn't speak with a decision-maker, I'd tell the person I talked with that I'd come back another time. When I left a product for a no obligation, one-week trial, I told them the day and approximate time I expected to return. I made a note of this and always kept my word. It was never a hard sell approach; I wouldn't have gotten involved if it was.

The challenge to sell Eagle 5000 units grabbed my attention. These were impressive 35-pound, commercial application-type, air purification units. They were perfect for use in bars and taverns, restaurants, hotels, bowling alleys and pet boarding facilities. The units were priced fairly and there were nice margins on them; a perfect win/win situation. Now, it was up to me to make businesses aware of them. I sold over two hundred of these babies in my time in this business. People couldn't believe it and would say, "how did you ever accomplish that?" I always had product in my car; I approached business decision-makers and I let them try one or more of the units in their environments for one week. The products did the rest…they worked and they worked well.

For four years we rented a space in the outdoor Fly Market during the annual, week long Experimental Aircraft Association Convention to demonstrate and sell our "state-of-the-art" air purifiers. This internationally attended event evolved into what is now called Air Venture. Our first summer exhibiting there was in 2003, and this was also only about three months after we began working the home-based business.

Julie and I worked early and long hours there, but we sure wouldn't trade the experience for anything. We rented the use of a large, well-secured tent (which they'd set up for us) and went to work hawking our wonderful products. We believed in them and that consistently came across to people who stopped by our tent. The venue itself was marvelous,

At our EAA tent in late July of 2005.

but the weather was often not as accommodating. The weeks were marked with days of extreme wind, heat and blustering rain.

We met a ton of awesome people there. This event was once known to draw three quarters of a million visitors each year. You can't sell shoes from an empty wagon. We knew if we were going to be at this event that we needed to have considerable product readily available for sale. Julie and I were rookies our first year there, but we were 'prepared to dance', as I've been known to say. We shared the tent space with a friend and fellow EcoQuest business owner. I wanted to make sure that potential customers would be able to touch and see the products and then take one or more along with them. The featured product weighed close to 20 pounds, but there were a couple of different options to chose from. We also kept a nice selection of colors available, and not just in pictures...we had them with us under the tent.

There was a slogan that we credit to fellow former EcoQuest business owner Leia Ryan from Minnesota. It is "stack 'em high and watch 'em fly." When people saw an abundance of product it lent further credibility to its importance. Every indoor environment needs at least one. What was it worth to be able to regularly be breathing in clean air when you were in your homes, businesses or vehicles. After all, most of us spend considerable portions of our lives indoors. Ironically, Leia had been an exhibitor at this annual convention for a number of years prior to us joining the business. She also had a booth inside one of the hangar locations that first year. We did well our first two years there, but weather conditions significantly impacted our performance each of the last two years and the grind of the one week commitment became too much when the pros and cons of having a booth at this event were evaluated. We did not wish to move to one of the vendor spots which were located inside of airplane hangars. They were extremely stuffy and we'd miss the enjoyment of watching the various activity taking place in the air.

Over the years we participated in a number of business and health expos, trade and home and garden shows, pet expos and women's fairs. I worked the business full-time and Julie would help me, whenever she was able to, in a limited capacity being a dedicated high school teacher. We normally carried on the tradition of "stack 'em high and watch 'em fly."

Gary and Julie at their booth at a Home-Garden Expo.

Working these shows was usually very enjoyable. Again, we met a lot of very nice people, a number of which became customers. If we'd see these people again at another show, they would always be most complimentary of the products and our customer service. It wasn't unusual for one of them to tell other people, who were at our booth at the time, that they would definitely recommend both us and our products. This became so gratifying because our credibility has and always will mean a great deal to us.

I am very proud of the meaning behind a term that I coined called "perpetual awareness." It stressed the fundamental importance of always being cognizant of why you were actually in this specific business. Air purifiers were the flagship products. Number one: you believed in these products; if you didn't, you shouldn't be involved with them. Number two: it was up to you to effectively communicate their value and importance to others. I used to teach this concept to our group and to others whenever possible. I was asked to be interviewed and recorded in order to provide a product retailing training disk to fellow colleagues. I remember being around strangers filling up with gas, riding in an elevator or standing in a parking lot whereby I would commonly say "It's a nice day today. I sure love what I do." There were many times when I'd hear, "what do you do?" I typically would have some product and a charged "living proof" demo unit nearby in my car. I placed a number of products for one week, no obligation trials this way. People could readily tell the passion that I had for what I was doing. I always protected myself by capturing sufficient contact information and had them sign and date a document before taking the serial numbered product. Did some of these trials turn into sales? Yes, they most certainly did and more often than you may think. Did I get burned doing this? No, I did not. Some times you have to think outside of the box.

We bought a lot of product over the years in this business. We had purchased and sold close to $500,000 worth of inventory. This is a pretty respectable amount for an old bean counter who had previously only sold a used Camaro on carsoup.com. I developed a sincere passion for this business because I believed in it and so did Julie. I fully expected to be involved with it for the rest of my working years. We wanted to turn it into something special. It sure was refreshing for quite some time.

With my deterioration in health, it was becoming noticeably harder and harder for me to carry products, remove most of them from boxes, set up and knock down display areas, etc. I could no longer safely climb even a two-step ladder. There was a specific time in Kaukauna when I did not think that I was going to be able to carry an Eagle unit up some stairs. I'm very thankful to have enjoyed this business for the time that I was able to enjoy it. I have no sour grapes. Who would have ever thought Lil Gar would be selling air purifiers in his lifetime….but I'll tell you this, if you're thinking of doing so, don't let me discourage you from STACKING 'EM HIGH and then WATCHING THEM FLY.

You Must Answer This

∞ 32 ∞
Thanks Phred...THIS COULD ONLY BE MANHATTAN

I was asked by an industry consultant to do a presentation on the use of benchmarking techniques to monitor a business' performance at the 13th annual Direct Marketing Association (DMA) convention in New York City in June of 1996. Fortunately, I was able to bring Julie along and we combined this trip with an unforgettable vacation that was to include both New York and Boston.

We'd never been to either city before, but we were actually the most excited about seeing Boston. We believed that the awesome city of Chicago did not deserve to take a back seat to New York. Rather, we thought that a disservice was being done by referring to it as the second city. Boy, were we wrong! There is absolutely no place like the Big Apple and the excitement and pulse of Manhattan is incredible.

Julie and I love visiting Chicago. Michigan Avenue during Christmas time is wonderful. It's a great place to walk and the food options are endless. Spending some time in Grant Park and seeing an afternoon baseball game at Wrigley Field is priceless. We've gone there with friends and always had a very good time. My kind of town...Chicago is.

When Phred Huber of Huber and Associates inquired about my interest in doing a presentation on her behalf at the DMA convention in New York City I was flattered. This was a great opportunity, and I was extremely interested in pursuing it. I would also be representing my company, Miles Kimball. My boss supported it and he was given the approval to authorize payment for my airfare and hotel accommodations for a couple of the days that I'd be spending in Manhattan. Thankfully, Julie was able to accompany me and we sandwiched a vacation around the presentation. Being a teacher, she was off from work during this time.

We landed at LaGuardia Airport on Saturday, June 22nd, and took a cab to our hotel in Manhattan. It was the New York Hilton and Towers and this

You Must Answer This

Speaker badge.

was where the convention was to be held. I had gotten us tickets to see the play "Les Miserables" at the Imperial Theatre on 45th Street that first evening. We had seen a few Broadway caliber plays before, but they were not on Broadway. This certainly didn't disappoint. The night was topped off nicely by us relaxing while having a glass of wine and a couple of tasty sandwiches at an impressive outdoor, corner bistro.

The next day we took the subway to Battery Park, a ferry to see the Statue of Liberty and marveled at the Twin Towers. There was so much to take in and not enough time to truly do it justice. We made sure to spend some quality time in Central Park while we were there and also took a peaceful horse-drawn carriage ride that began near its entryway. This is a great city to walk in and tying in the use of the subway system enables you to see a good deal more. We enjoyed our first Broadway play so much that we got in line to purchase discount tickets for a 6:30 p.m. performance of "Beauty and the Beast" at the Palace Theatre that very same evening. The magic of Time Square, the garment district, riding the original escalator at Macy's, visiting St. Patrick's Cathedral and taking the double deck bus tour of the city all left their remarkable and indelible impressions on us.

Monday was the start of the DMA convention. My presentation was scheduled to take place on Tuesday afternoon from 1:45 until 3:00 p.m. That first day, we found the location of the meeting room. Everything

The two Broadway plays we went to.

that I needed was already there and it was ready to go. I completed a brief rehearsal. We then headed down to the Exhibit Hall and talked with a number of the vendors who were there. Kathy, from R.R. Donnelly, invited us to a cocktail party they were sponsoring the

Julie and Gary at an outdoor cafe in Rockeller Center in 1996.

next evening in the Rainbow Room on the 65th floor of 30 Rockefeller Center. We were a customer of theirs and she also bought us lunch at the historical Rosie O'Grady's restaurant on 7th Avenue.

There were clearly a lot of people attending this convention and I was excited about Tuesday. Julie came along for encouragement and took a place in the audience. I was pleased that there was a solid turnout. The presentation included a slide show and it was very well received. I felt personally satisfied and professionally appreciated. The feedback I was given was very positive and reinforcing. It seemed like icing on the cake that evening when we were in the prestigious Rainbow Room. The view from there was incredible! We were leaving for Boston the next evening, but we'd already experienced enough of Manhattan to be completely sold on it.

Being a long-time major league baseball fan, I'd always wanted to see games at Fenway Park and Yankee Stadium. I was able to secure tickets for a game in each place before we left. I excitedly got tickets for the Tigers and Red Sox and the Orioles and Yankees. We took the short shuttle flight to Boston on Wednesday evening and stayed in the suburb of Braintree. I'd also gotten us tickets for a Boston Pops 'Swing Night' concert for the subsequent Saturday. I knew that Julie would appreciate this. We went into town the three days we were there via the T subway system. This gave us the opportunity to do many things in Boston. We comfortably walked the memorable Freedom Trail and spent some time inside the historic Old North Church.

Gary and the Green Monster inside Fenway Park.

Late that first afternoon, we took a cab ride to Fenway. Our tickets were for that evening's game. The 'Big Dig' was well underway at this time and there was some other road construction going on around this area too. He was only able to drop us off relatively nearby. That was okay though. I was hyperventilating as we approached the venerable 'Fenway' from behind the infamous Green Monster. How could one ever forget the large, lighted Citgo sign? It was raining off and on during the game. Our seats were down the right field line and we could easily see into the Detroit Tigers' bullpen. I distinctly remember telling Julie to watch the movement on former Brewers pitcher Mike Myers' pitches as he was warming up. The Tigers ended up winning the game 9 to 6. We saw stars Mo Vaughn, Jose Canseco (who walked four times in the game) and Cecil Fielder. Needless to say, I bought a Fenway Frank.

The next day I wanted to get back to Fenway to get some pictures taken. Unbelievably, we were actually able to get inside the park and walk around. I was able to take a bunch of pictures. I got out by the thirty seven foot high Monster, looked down into the Red Sox dugout and contemplated the history of this stand alone monument to major league baseball. I'll never forget this. We were not bothered, rushed or inhibited. Right across from the stadium we could see and here a sports talk radio show that was in progress. There was also a memorabilia store next door. We stopped in and Julie bought me an autographed Carl Yastrzemski baseball as a belated birthday gift. He is one of my all-time favorite players. I bought a Red Sox cap there as well.

Later, it was a treat visiting the original Cheers. This also seemed like a 'must see' for us. We were also able to get to the Public Garden and see the swan boats. We enjoyed Quincy Market and the marketplace at Faneuil Hall. This city is full of history and if we had to do it over again, we would prefer to stay right in Boston.

We headed back to New York the next day, after a late night, on a very early flight. We hadn't gotten much sleep and were both absolutely exhausted. The feather bed in the Omni hotel room on 3rd Avenue and 52nd Street was about as inviting as one could possibly be. Our Yankees/ Orioles game tickets were for that afternoon and it was raining pretty hard all morning. As bad as I wanted to see a game played at Yankee Stadium, we made the right decision and chose to pass on attending this one. We actually believed it might be rained out anyway, or at least significantly interrupted by rain. We learned later that the game was able to be played and completed.

We left New York with no regrets and looked forward to coming back. Mid-town Manhattan had the most electricity of any area either of us had ever experienced before. There's a steady pulse there that is both highly invigorating and exciting.

Another nice opportunity was to surface later when Phred Huber asked me to be a co-presenter with her, as part of a two-person panel, at the National Conference on Operations and Fulfillment (NCOF) to be held in Orlando, Florida in April of 1998. It was conducted at a brand new Disney resort hotel. I received a letter dated May 18th from the NCOF's Vice President of Conferences, Robin Altman. It was regarding the quality of our presentation that was entitled Case Study: How Two Catalog Companies Use Benchmarks To Manage Their Costs. She was very complimentary in saying, "I am pleased to inform you that the attendees at that session gave you a score of 85%, which rates as a very good score. Gary, again, thanks for a job well done."

This conference came during the same time that Disney was also to unveil its new Animal Kingdom complex. Phred and I were able to be there when it first opened its gates. It was very impressive and comedian Drew Carey was on the grounds making a featured appearance. It's interesting when the circumstances surrounding one opportunity in our lives open up a door to enable us to take advantage of other opportunities. This speaking invitation came as an aftermath from the success of my earlier presentation.

Thanks to Phred, Julie and I were able to experience New York City for the very first time. On our own, we probably would not have hurried to get there. Another important lesson that was learned here is that one should not make influential judgments without having a sound basis for making such judgments. The Big Apple resoundingly speaks for itself if you take the opportunity to listen. There's a part of this jewel of a city which will be in the forefront of our memories forever. THIS COULD ONLY BE MANHATTAN.

ೞ 33 ഔ
I'LL NEVER FORGET THAT SMELL

My first and only previous visit to New York City was in the summer of 1996. It was before the tragedies of 9/11 and the World Trade Center stood proudly near the banks of the Hudson River. Julie and I stood on the shore across from the Twin Towers on a nice, sunny day and took a picture of their distinctive majesty. Little did we imagine what was to take place just over five years from this time.

The horrific terrorist attacks caused cancellation of a football game scheduled fo Sunday, September 16, 2001, between the Green Bay Packers and the New York Giants. Friend and former co-worker Bob Snyder and myself had been invited to attend this game. It was rescheduled for Sunday, January 6, 2002, and the offer we'd been given still stood. Bob and I had made alternative plans in order to get there. The night before, we took the subway down to Ground Zero and spent considerable time walking around and talking with other people who were in this area.

The accounts payable function came under my responsibility as Corporate Controller at Miles Kimball Company. There was a time when vendors were commonly paid on a 2% ten/net 30 basis. Effective cash management became more and more of an important issue and my boss and I attended one of the annual treasury

Gary with the Twin Towers in the background in June of 1996.

management conferences in Chicago in the summer of 2000. We both attended a presentation that was done by a gentleman who preached strategic cash management and the value to be realized from improving a company's monetary float position. We consciously aimed at converting most of our vendors over to a 60-day payment cycle. This was difficult to fully implement because a number of the vendors were fairly small.

My reputation and credibility were always extremely important to me. I believe that respect is earned and people usually knew what I stood for. My father was that type of person and I've never lost sight of its significance. I had previously developed solid relationships with most of our vendors. They came to know that they could rely on what I'd told them and when I committed to doing something, I'd do my best to ensure that it happened.

One of the many vendors I'd developed a mutual respect with was Fred Levine of Carmen Products in New York. I found Fred to be a likeable, straight-shooter who appreciated honesty and integrity. He was the President of the company and even though I'd enforced some tighter restrictions and guidelines, he respected where I was coming from. He knew that my word was good.

After the company was purchased by an investment banking firm, they immediately took control of a number of specific facets of the business. Early on, payables were to be stretched to 90-day terms. There were not to be any exceptions. This was communicated to vendors and their basic response was: we're going to have difficulty accommodating this and still be a responsive partner for your operation. In time, a number of vendor terms were directed to be changed to 120 days.

We all usually remember where we were when certain major events took place in our lives. Hand in hand with this are memories of what we were doing at the time or who we may have been talking to. Interestingly, with some events many of our associated memories are at least partially blanked out and effectively erased. A case in point is: I cannot recall any specifics from the life threatening car accident I was involved in in 1979 between the time I first turned my steering wheel to the right to avoid the collision, then quickly turning it back to the left after hitting a chuckhole in the side of the road. The next thing I remember is waking up in a hospital emergency room bed in Neenah, Wisconsin.

On Tuesday morning, September 11, 2001, I was in my office at Miles Kimball in Oshkosh. My boss came in my office around 8:30 and said he'd heard that a plane had just crashed into one of the towers at the World Trade Center. Like many of you, we were at a loss to explain why such a thing could have happened. There must have been some major engine malfunction or equipment failures. Did the pilot have a heart attack or were there other distractions in the cockpit which caused this type of thing to take place?

Needless to say, we all know now what happened to cause this to unfold. It was the first of four coordinated terrorist strikes on our soil. Two hours later both of the towers of the Trade Center had collapsed. The fallout from these attacks killed or injured numerous people and was to impact the lives of their respective families forever. Resulting fires and residual debris caused heavy damage to the entire complex and surrounding area. Buildings in the immediate vicinity suffered major structural issues. There were those that experienced some form of collapse.

I'll never forget seeing these Ground Zero tributes either.

I'd graciously been invited by Fred Levine to attend the Packers vs. Giants game scheduled to be played on Sunday, September 16, 2001. He said to bring a friend as he had four season tickets for this game to be played at MetLife Stadium in the Meadowlands Complex of East Rutherford, New Jersey. I invited (huge Packers fan) Bob Snyder to go with me and we'd paid for plane tickets and a hotel reservation in Newark.

The implications of 9/11 created a scary time for all of us. This was foreign stuff for everyone to process. I appreciated it when Fred told me that his offer for us to attend the game held, if we were still interested. My wife was reluctant to have me go but by the end of the year things had calmed down quite a bit. Bob and I flew out on Saturday, January 5th. We'd gotten a flight into Newark, which was the same airport where one of the hi-jacked terrorist flights had left from in the early morning of September 11th.

We decided to take a speed train into New York City that evening. We then took the subway to lower Manhattan and Ground Zero. It looked like a war zone area there with large stanchions of temporary lighting all over the place. There were numerous memorial displays featuring flowers and photos of people who were killed during and after the attacks. Police and firemen were seen walking throughout this area and we talked with a number of them. There was an eerie feeling of despair that had clearly remained here. An

Bob and Gary at Giants Stadium before the game.

overriding smell in the air clearly got and kept our attention. One fireman told us that the smell was so strong that it fully permeated an eight block area for a long time…and here it was nearly four months later.

The Packers won the game 34-25, but there was a major controversy which took place during it. This resulted when Giants star Michael Strahan set the all-time single game sacks record at 22 1/2. For 57 minutes of the 60-minute game, Strahan had not gotten a sack against Packers quarterback Brett Favre. Then with just under three minutes to go in the game, it clearly appeared during a play that Favre simply fell down and gave him the sack needed to break the prior record.

Bob and I attempted to return the favor by offering to treat Fred and one of his friends from New York to see a Packers/Giants game played in Lambeau Field. Thankfully, we were able to do so on Sunday afternoon, October 3, 2004. He and a friend came in on Saturday. Julie and I met up with them for an enjoyable evening visit and dinner at Lombardi's Supper Club in Appleton.

I always kid about remembering the late morning smell on Bourbon Street in New Orleans. The heat on the blacktop brings out a very memorable and seemingly unique odor. But after spending considerable

Ground Zero tribute in January of 2002.

time at Ground Zero on Saturday evening, January 5, 2002, I'LL NEVER BE ABLE TO FORGET THAT SMELL. I don't even know how to describe it, but it was strong and it was very unpleasant. For me, it represents an unforgettable reminder to what's referred to as "the greatest tragedy ever on American soil."

🕮 34 🕮
HAPPY BIRTHDAY
To You My Friend

Many years ago I worked in an environment where the daily stress level could be cut with a knife. When someone brought in a treat for their birthday, the atmosphere would dramatically improve for about the time it took to finish a ten-minute break. This was a volatile division of a large international company which was having major financial issues. I've learned over the years that the personality of an organization's leader permeates the environment of the entire organization.

I was nearly killed in an automobile accident back in March of 1979 and have learned to try to appreciate every day of my life. This accident occurred after I'd left the toxic environment. I believe that consistently keeping things in perspective should be one of the most important objectives in each of our lives.

I was born on Sunday, June 21, 1953. It was the first day of summer, the longest day of the year and also happened to be Father's Day. My Dad had turned 47 in May and my original conception came as quite the surprise. As I'd referenced earlier, when my mother was told by the doctor that she was pregnant she told him, "I can't be pregnant." He turned to her and said "don't look at me, I had nothing to do with it."

When I was a little kid, my brother Doug loved teasing his baby brother. I'd be sitting in a high chair and he'd take a hat and toss it on my head...causing it to spin around. This would cause me

Gary on pedal horse from Doug and Shirley.

Santa Doug and Gary.

to giggle for awhile. He also gave me the nickname of "peachie ween." He and my sister-in-law were so proud of their unexpected brother; he was nearly 24 when I was born. Doug used to say that we were 24 years apart in age, but I'd quickly counter that it was only 23-1/2.

They were always trying to surprise me with something. He played a very believable Santa for me for a number of years. It was frustrating because my only brother always had to work late on Christmas Eve! I'd always do a little jig before opening my presents. One year they bought me a unique pedal horse and carriage that they'd seen when visiting Chicago.

I had a very good childhood and even though my parents were much older, it wasn't that apparent to me growing up. I was pretty easy going and was also pretty spoiled. Thanks to my parents, I learned early on to respect others. "Please" and "thank you" has always come easy to me and I still look to open and hold doors open for people I encounter. Watching my wonderful Dad go

RAINBOW PARK

The
LIT'L GAR
"3-ZIPPER SALUTE"

SATURDAY, JUNE 18TH
12:00 TO 8:30
—FREE BEER AND HELLO—

(BE PREPARED TO SMILE!)

Gary

The 3-Zipper Salute birthday party invitation template in 83.

through his health issues was hard on me, but it also has made me stronger. It's enabled me to appreciate the little things and be more cognizant of what's really important.

I loved celebrating my birthday. My mother would invite friends over to join us for a party with balloons and cake that would always be fun and light-hearted. Thanks to my Mom, as time went on, I would have an annual outdoor party on the Saturday before or after my birthday. Being during the summer, we'd play volleyball and wiffle ball and she always made plenty of tasty Spanish hamburgers. Later, park shelters, beer kegs and sound systems were involved. There were some memorable ones alright. No one who'd attended would forget the

Gary drumming at his 50th birthday party.

Rainbow 29er, the 3-Zipper Salute or the Treaty of the 3s. One of the best things I always enjoyed about the parties was seeing my friends together and watching them having fun while sharing their day with me.

The pattern continued after I got married. Julie always fusses for my birthday. We've had all-day Saturday parties with both live and canned outdoor entertainment and commonly volleyball. There've been special cakes featuring a replicated photo of a young Gary holding a baseball bat, a drum set and Milwaukee Brewers and Packers logos. For my 50th birthday, she rented the same hall where our wedding reception was held. Julie was able to have some musicians from one of my favorite area rock bands play for it…once known as the one and only Billy Shears. They did a version of the Beatles' song "Eleanor Rigby" that was absolutely sensational. They were in the process of retooling and their new name was Casting Cleos. I was even able to drum a few songs with the band that night, talk about leaving me with some awesome memories!

Julie sent this email to the band the following week:
Hi "Casting Cleos" (a.k.a. The Awesome Rockers),

I just wanted to "thank you" again for making Gary Beyer's BIG FIVE-O birthday bash on June 21st a smashing success! Lit'l Gar as he is affectionately called by his many friends, has always been a lover of

good ROCK music. Needless to say, having you guys play your wonderful brand of "kick ___" rock-n-roll was a dream come true for him and brought back many great memories of The Billy Shears days!!! I also know Gary was thrilled to drum along to a few songs. He has been talking about it ever since! Thanks again for an awesome, rockin' evening!:)

Lit'l Gar's "Better Half",

Julie Beyer

I love planning these types of parties for others too. I was able to surprise my mother on her 70th birthday and Julie on her 40th. Well, at least I almost surprised Julie. She was somehow able to get an inkling about this prior to it taking place. Thankfully, she didn't let on and still had a great time.

Another surprise on Julie's 40th birthday.

The annual celebrations have been curtailed since the passing of my mother and brother. A daily expression of our thanks and gratitude remains. In fact, this desire has become even more prominent for both Julie and myself. As we get older, we better appreciate the simplest of things. We do not take our many blessings for granted.

Stress is a different animal. A reasonable degree of it keeps us sharp and on our toes. Too much of it impacts us in destructive ways, some of which are inobvious in their effect(s). We all handle stressful situations and circumstances differently. What is most important is that we each find effective ways to counter balance our stress. My brother used to say, "don't let things overwhelm you."

I consciously developed a habit of saying "happy birthday" to co-workers over the years. Some residue from the automobile accident was that I found it to be more important to give daily thanks for the blessings in our lives. Celebrating one's birthday annually was fine, but recognizing the significance of one's daily existence also seemed appropriate. I would say "happy birthday" to co-workers I'd encounter when passing them in a hallway. I'd usually receive one of three distinct reactions; "it's not my birthday" or "huh?" or as time went on I'd get, "happy birthday to you." Regardless, if it jogged someone's mind off the stress of their day for only a few seconds, I'd accomplished my real intention. What got funny is there were times that I'd forget to say it and invariably this was on the day of a person's celebrated birthday. It commonly got to a point where co-workers would do the same to me and, at some of these times, they'd catch me deep in thought as well

I once had a General Manager, whom I highly respected, tell me in a third floor bathroom at work that he was impressed with how I dealt with people. To this day, it is one of the most treasured compliments I've ever received. I still believe in the saying "life is to be lived." It sounds so simple, but both self-imposed and uncontrollable restrictions and circumstances regularly complicate this effort for us. The next time you're celebrating your birthday I ask you to reflect on what this truly means. When someone says "happy birthday" to you, I encourage you to respond, "HAPPY BIRTHDAY to you as well my friend." If you become so inclined, you should be readily able to reconcile their confusion.

You Must Answer This

❧ 35 ❧
WHAT HAPPENS IN VEGAS Cannot

JUST simply stay in Vegas. You can't help but bring many of your experiences from there back with you when you leave. Sure, they come in the form of memories, but what some memories! I remember a friend of mine telling me one time that I needed to get to Las Vegas. He could not believe that I hadn't been there before and I was in my forties at that point. I basically had no interest in ever going.

In the summer of 1999, Julie and I decided to finally check out Las Vegas. Being a huge Star Trek fan, Julie really wanted to see the Star Trek Experience that began being featured at the Hilton in January of 1998. This was enough to entice her to go. Where this was at didn't matter; she would have wanted to see it, regardless.

I've never been much of a gambler. I enjoy playing some Black Jack once in a while, but have never been truly hooked on it. Going to the dog track was always fun for me though. The same friend, Bob Heidke (whom I referenced above regarding never being in Las Vegas before) and I visited the track that was in our area from time to time. That venue didn't stay open very long. Once it closed, we'd occasionally visit another track that was located south of Milwaukee. Neither of us would bet very much, but it was always an enjoyable time.

Julie's a good sport, but she is not a fan of gambling. She'll play some video poker if we're in a casino, but will not go out of her way to play any of the machines that are commonly found there. In other words, neither of us would seem to be legitimate prospects for the Las Vegas scene. We had only considered Vegas to be a place for obsessive gamblers, mesmerizing lights and over-embellished hype. We aren't into smoke and mirrors and we had envisioned this so-called "Sin City" to be little more than that.

Prior to leaving, I attempted to come up with a game plan. We'd always heard that four days was enough time to spend in Vegas. We were leaving on August 12th and would be returning on the 16th. Never seeing a Cirque du Soleil show, we were most intrigued to get to one while visiting there. We were to be staying on 'the Strip' at the New York New York complex. We had no intentions of renting a car and expected to do considerable walking. August was not the ideal time to be out there, but with Julie being a full-time teacher...any trips we'd take were usually during the summer or when she'd have a longer Easter break. I got us tickets to see "Mystere" at Treasure Island the first night that we were to be there. We checked into the hotel, got our bearings somewhat and took a cab over to the show. What a way to begin a Vegas vacation. It was incredible!

Flying into Las Vegas is quite the eye opener. This astonishing city just appears out of nowhere. Nothing, nothing...whoa!...and this is during the daytime. When the lights of the city are on, you feel like you're heading into a fantasyland. You are; and it's an adult fantasyland. When we landed, we each could feel the excitement building in us. We weren't thinking about gambling, but we were thinking about seeing the sights that were there. The cab ride to our hotel, alone was invigorating. The various marquis' couldn't help but catch our eyes, as they are intended to.

This city has such a strong pulse that you can't help but feel it. That certainly stays in Vegas because there is no way to replicate it back home; or probably anywhere else for that matter. While you're there though, it grabs and keeps your attention. We'd been to Manhattan and were caught off guard by how it had captured us. The same thing was happening in Las Vegas; a totally different city, yet, we were fooled again. This city was so much more than gambling, lights and hype. It was exciting to be there. We literally felt like we'd been transferred to a one-of-a-kind place that provided a fantasy-like experience for us.

Julie was awed by the Star Trek exhibit. We proceeded to take in as much as we could during our week there. We did some gambling, but we were more into the shows and the extensive live entertainment. We'd gotten advance tickets for "Lord of the Dance", which was featured at New York New York. It was spectacular and we found it to be exhausting just sitting there watching the performance. The plentiful replicas from the Big Apple were impressive; the mini-Brooklyn bridge, the Statue of Liberty and Central Park were each nicely represented.

I'd also gotten us advance tickets to see Siegfried and Roy at The Mirage. The tickets were for Sunday night and we were to be leaving the next day. It was a spellbinding magic show which featured the incorporation of numerous live tigers. How improbable is that? Tragically, a few years later, Roy Horn was

Siegfried and Roy at the Mirage.

critically injured during one of their shows. We made it a point to check out most of the other casino complexes that were located on 'the Strip.' There certainly was nothing like this around us. We were ready to go home by the end of our stay there, but we knew that we'd be back.

Little did we expect that we'd be heading back to Las Vegas to celebrate the arrival of the new century. This wasn't even five months later. A co-worker, Steve Vestal, and myself had talked about this. He and his wife Becky had been to Vegas before, but they hadn't been there in awhile. I had told him how impressed Julie and I had been during our one and only visit. We thought, what better place to be to bring in the 21st century. Like many people, we were a bit concerned with the issues being discussed during this time. Would automated systems adjust, would it be safe to be there, etc. when the year actually changed over from 1999 to 2000.

We were planning on going there together, but work demands caused Steve and Becky to alter their plans. Julie and I had previously never traveled anywhere during the last week of the year. We decided to leave the day after Christmas and were to be staying at the Imperial Palace in the heart of the Strip. What truly made up our minds was when I was able to get advance tickets in early September to see the band The Eagles and minstrel storyteller Jackson Browne play at the Mandalay Events Center on December 29th. This was during the "Millennium Tour." The Eagles are one of our favorite, if not our very favorite, band(s) and to see them fronted by Jackson Browne seemed too good to be true.

```
Confirmation #        1-51180  Performance Date:29-DEC-99

Tix  Order
Qty  Date      Performance Name          Sec.   Row   Seat(s)
---  -------   ---------------           ----   ---   -------
  2  11-SEP-99 (LV) EAGLES+JACKSON BROWN  L112    C    1-2




         GARY L BEYER
         2399 GOLDEN AVE                      TOTAL FACE VAL
         OSHKOSH,WI 54904-7970
```
Eagles and Jackson Browne concert confirmation December 29, 1999.

Prior to celebrating the arrival of the new century, we ended up counting down the passage of time inside The Mirage on New Year's Eve. We were given the coolest champagne glasses in our room which commemorated our being at the 'IP' hotel at this momentous time. The stems of the glasses feature a 'cut out' of the number 2000. These certainly weren't left in Vegas either.

We were hooked. Between 2000 and 2005 we went back to Las Vegas three more times. Rita Rudner was at her best when we saw her act at New York New York in August of 2001. We bought her book and I had her autograph it for us after the show. Unfortunately, Julie had gotten sick during the show and was in the bathroom. I waited in line, but Julie wasn't able to return in time. In August of 2002, we saw comedian Judy Tenuta's irreverent, but hilarious, show at The Improv inside of Harrah's. George Wallace was excellent in July of 2004 at The Flamingo Showroom.

The musicals "Chicago" and "Mamma Mia." were both enjoyed at Mandalay Bay. Abba's songs went through each of our heads for the next month. I'm a huge Al Green fan and we saw him perform at the Paris Las Vegas Showroom in August of 2002. Unfortunately, his voice seemed to be having some issues that evening. He passed out tons of red roses to the ladies who were in the audience.

Our third time there we made it a point to take a cab over to the original Las Vegas. Getting off of the Strip was a definite change of pace. It was neat seeing the Fremont Street Experience and visiting places like Circus Circus and The Four Queens, but once was enough for us. This was not the case, however, with regard to the Star Trek Experience. We revisited it in mid-

July of 2004 and this time, Julie got to sit in the captain's chair and have her picture taken.

There was an occasion, as we were on a crosswalk heading to The Venetian, when we crossed paths with the one and only Shaquille O'Neal. It was like…that was Shaq! I'll never forget that he was walking between two friends and had plaid shorts on. He towered over these friends and they were probably each close to six feet tall. We were told inside the casino that he was staying there at that time.

We identified a couple of favorite places to stay in Vegas. The Aladdin became a hotel of choice. It was our place of residence for two consecutive years. The attached Desert Passage Shops were fun to visit. Our most comfortable spot became Harrah's. We stayed there our last two years. It was just so cozy and unassuming. The doors were usually open and you could play Black Jack while being close to the sidewalk of 'the Strip.' I'll never forget singing the Eagles' song "Tequila Sunrise", one late afternoon during karaoke at a place that was located in the front of Harrah's. It was a lot of fun. Their complex featured an entertaining outdoor carnival-like atmosphere with a large, canopied oval-shaped bar, numerous kiosks and a very inviting Ghirardelli chocolate and ice cream shop. This latter option, especially, kept calling our names.

We were able to see a total of three different Cirque du Soleil shows there. In addition to "Mystere", we saw "KA" at the MGM Grand and the Beatles' "Love" at The Mirage. They all were exceptional. Being huge Beatles fans, we're still enjoying the "Love" DVD. Words do not do justice when attempting to describe these shows to anyone. It's best to say that you just need to see them for yourselves. I had experienced Blue Man Group in Chicago, but Julie never had. This became an enjoyable evening for us at The Luxor in August of 2002.

Another of our most memorable trips to Las Vegas came in late June of 2006. Julie became a huge fan of the four-man singing group known as IL Divo. I found out that they were going to be performing on the 23rd at the Mandalay Bay Events Center. I surprised Julie with tickets for this concert and she was absolutely thrilled to be able to see them. They didn't disappoint. We had a couple of friends who lived in nearby Henderson. It was great being able to hook up with them when we were there. In the

Gary meeting drummer great Carl Palmer of Emerson, Lake & Palmer fame.

process of walking past the House of Blues at Mandalay Bay the next afternoon, we noticed a sign advertising the fact that Carl Palmer and his band were to be playing there on the evening of June 24th. I said, "Carl Palmer is going to be playing here tonight?" Being a long-admiring fan of his, and being a fellow drummer, I was shocked to find out that this revered legend from Emerson, Lake and Palmer fame was to be playing there with his new band. We were able to get four front row tickets and decided to stay around this general area longer than we had planned. After the concert I was able to meet him and have him autograph a tour shirt for me. I was like a little kid!

Las Vegas is full of surprises. There was another afternoon during this particular stay that Julie and I were walking through The Forum Shops at Caesar's Palace. We were passing a Field of Dreams store and thankfully, Julie was paying more attention than I was. There was a short line outside and she looked inside and spotted this guy signing autographs at a table. It

was none other than Pete Rose, baseball's all-time hits king. I could not believe it. Here, he's nearby, signing autographs and having pictures taken. We were totally surprised by this and needless to say, we got in line to go inside. I bought a nice photo of him and had him personalize it for me. Fortunately, I had our camera along and Julie took a couple of pictures of Pete and myself; which I will always treasure. The odds of this happening couldn't have been very good. I had the opportunity to talk with him

Gary and the great Pete Rose.

for a few minutes too. For this to happen, to a huge baseball fan like myself, was incredible. Was it just a coincidence that we happened to walk by at the time he was there?...I don't believe so. It's not as if there's so little going on in Vegas and it's such a spontaneous city.

Our last trip there was in the summer of 2007. Like our venture to New York City and into Manhattan in particular, we were pleasantly caught by surprise by this enticing city. Our expectations were pretty low before we arrived. It didn't take either of us very long before we realized that many of our unenlightened assumptions were erroneous. Our first-hand experiences with these two incredible cities taught us an important lesson: be careful when making judgments on things you haven't been able to experience for yourselves. Las Vegas is so much more than just gambling, bright lights and over-embellished hype. Hopefully, we'll be able to get back there again sometime, but regardless of this WHAT HAPPENS IN VEGAS CANNOT JUST STAY IN VEGAS. It would be a terrible disservice to this city if that were actually the case. The wonderful memories, which we make while we are there, must always return home with us.

You Must Answer This

ರ 36 ಬ
MY GREATEST BLESSING!!

We will all go through difficult things in our lives. Some will be faced with more than others. There will be those that are extremely challenging and those that will be much easier to get beyond. A time will come when we each of us are chosen to leave this earth. What truly matters is how we spend the period we are blessed with between our birth and our inevitable death.

I've been nearly killed in a car accident, extremely disillusioned after calling off a wedding, spared serious injury from a major work explosion, exasperated from trying to help an incredible mother dealing with steadily progressive Alzheimers, unnervingly helpless watching my admired father suffer through the onslaught of colon cancer, incredibly forlorn in seeing my courageous brother lose his battle with cirrhosis of the liver, frequently disgruntled in the corporate world after being effected by decisions which impacted our ability to satisfy financial obligations and far too close to becoming blind in both eyes. Despite these disturbing things I believe that my life has been, and continues to be, exceptionally blessed.

You've read earlier that I'd don't believe in entitlement. It can become a curse for many people. To expect something to take place because we feel it is owed to us reveals a type of insecurity. We may even feel unworthy of being able to help make some things happen through our own merits. A belief that 'my effort doesn't really matter anyway' is not only self-defeating, but effectively stagnating. We play an important role in the blessings we are to receive.

Interwoven within each of the disturbing things above are considerable blessings. Here are just some of them. The car accident taught me to be more mindful of the responsibilities associated with driving a motorized vehicle. Being involved in an increasingly tenuous relationship, which nearly resulted in my wedding, gave me considerable cause to better analyze other potentially serious relationships. Learning that my staff and I likely avoided being injured or possibly even killed at work because an explosion occurred at its least likely time, during the early morning when we were not there, gave me reason to appreciate the people around me all the more. Throughout the years, I always saw my mother as this resilient and highly formidable person who could successfully take on nearly any challenge. A blessing that was resoundingly sent to me is that I have an even better recognition of the fact that we are all fragile beings. Growing up in an environment where my father was battling health issues taught me humility and an appreciation for a person's inner strength and character. The way my brother handled his inexorable struggles gave me a tremendous sense of pride in the fact that he was my brother. How could I ever forget this? Most of us take our sight for granted. I did before my problems with diplopia. Four subsequent and successful cataract and retinal-associated surgeries have further changed my perspective in this regard. The various job related issues have helped make me a more developed person. I take less and less for granted over the years and find myself much more aware of the sheer divinity of things around me.

The most important thing, that I do not take for granted, is my relationship with Julie. She is most definitely **MY GREATEST BLESSING!!** Julie is truly my soul mate. We've become each other's best friend and have

Gary and Julie at the Paine.

always enjoyed each other's company and support. We believe that we were meant to meet and our doing so was a major Godincidence. We're convinced that this meeting was so much bigger than our associated efforts, but we also recognize that it was these efforts which facilitated our opportunity to meet.

We've been comfortable with each other since we first met. Our communication has never been strained and we don't play games with each other. We commonly find that we could begin and end each other's thoughts and sentences. There are times when one of us will make a comment and the other will say, "you must have read my mind...I was just thinking that (or about to say that)." We typically view circumstances and situations in a very similar way. It's rare when we interpret something differently.

Not long after we were going together, Julie asked me the question, "what do you want out of life?" Needless to say, this is a pretty profound question. My answer to it was simply this, "I just want to be happy." What? Here, I was in a responsible job as a plant controller for a manufacturing company in town. I had an MBA and I equated being successful with being happy. This was because I'd thankfully already learned what is most important in each of our lives. There's an old saying that 'money cannot buy happiness' and I believe this is so true.

I've always been somewhat of a complex individual. I'm very much of an extrovert, but need some time to just keep for myself. I do not let a lot of people get very close to me. This isn't because I have anything to hide, but I'm protective of my privacy. I don't like it when outsiders get to feel so comfortable that they invade, what should be, private space. This goes for family, friends, neighbors and used car salesmen. On the other hand, when I feel very comfortable with someone, I treasure the opportunity to get closer to them. Julie and I are extremely close and that's definitely the way we both prefer it in our marriage. We don't believe in secrets from each other; except when it comes to birthdays or anniversaries.

I've found Julie to be a very deep and exceedingly intelligent person. Her retention of things is second to none. She exhibits a child-like enthusiasm for many things and I love that trait in her. I'm a highly sensitive person and she's always made me feel very loved and appreciated. We've found that our level of respect for each other is very high. We also trust each other implicitly. She continues to be a joy for me to be around. I'm also extremely proud of her.

Gary and Julie dancing at their wedding reception in 1988.

Julie's in her 34th year of teaching high school English. She's incredibly good at what she does. Her ability to reach kids is exceptional because she tries to meet them where they're at. Her style is no nonsense and she's a disciplinarian with expectations, but the kids know she's both fair and will respect them as individuals. We commonly run into former students of Julie's throughout the Valley over the years, and it's very clear to me that she made a good impression with them, even some of the more difficult ones. From Mrs. Beyer they learn more than Sophomore English curriculum, they also learn some important things which will help them the rest of their respective lives.

Neither of us are particularly superstitious, but it's amazing how often the number 13 has been interwoven in our life together. It's actually seen as kind of a lucky number for us. I called off a wedding on Friday the 13th. Interestingly, Julie's class room number when we first met turned out to be thirteen. We first visited New York City in June of 1996 when I was asked to be one of the featured speakers at the 13th annual Direct Marketing Association convention there. There've been other times when the number thirteen has shown up prominently in various situations or circumstances that we've found ourselves in. How about this? We've even celebrated our 25th wedding anniversary in the year 2013.

We've identified 'our special song.' It's "So Happy Together", which was written by The Turtles back in 1967. They even play it at Miller Park during Brewers baseball games. We both love music and have taken the opportunity to go to numerous concerts over our years together. Julie is also a very accomplished violinist. She held the first chair position for awhile in her high school orchestra. I've surprised her with a free-standing keyboard to tinker with as well. Like my brother Doug, I've played the drums for many years.

I believe that one of the neatest things anyone can possibly say about two people that have gotten married is that they're good for each other. Julie and I are good for each other. I know that other people who know us would quickly say this as well. No two people are completely alike…and that's a good thing. Partners bring different things to the table in every relationship. We both learn from and consistently grow with each other. For example, her love of classical music has broadened my musical horizons. My love of professional baseball has given her associated knowledge, to the point where she is comfortably able to talk some baseball with more serious fans. We may not share all of each other's interests, but we respect each of them. It makes us feel good when we can help satisfy one of the other one's interests.

I love Julie with all of my heart and there could never be a bigger blessing in my life. On October 1, 2013, we were married 25 years. We met a bit later in our lives and have no children of our own, but we are very grateful to God for bringing us together. She clearly is MY GREATEST BLESSING!!

Gary and Julie at Doug and Shirley's early in their marriage.

You Must Answer This

❧ In Closing ❧
DON'T GIVE UP...
YOU CAN'T GIVE UP

How many times have you heard the phrase "all things happen for a reason" (or some other version of it)? Whether you agree or disagree with this concept doesn't matter. Hopefully, one or more of the honest and true stories I've shared with you, from my own life, will at least have given you some food for thought.

My intent is not to convince you one way or the other. It's because I believe that such determination is strictly up to you. We each will be involved with varied events, experiences, encounters and circumstances which will take place during our lives. It's how we respond to and from them that creates the numerous stories that we could share with others.

I've come to believe that there are no coincidences in our lives. I used to use this word all the time and it seemed sufficient to explain something that had happened or else would justify something that was about to happen. It was irrelevant whether the subject of the explanation involved more serious issues or simply just inconsequential matters.

I contend that Julie and I were meant to meet and share our lives together. Part of my destiny was to write and submit the very specific and forthright ad which triggered her level of interest. Part of her destiny was to read my ad and hear the calming, androgynous voice which told her "you must answer this." This is what triggered Julie to write and submit her response. Importantly, timing implications were supportive and we each took the necessary actions which enabled us to take advantage of the life-changing opportunity which God had already facilitated. The resultant meshing of variables was to interweave both of our lives. I was born later in my parents' lives for some very important reasons. Many of these reasons could not have been detectable at that time, but they've become more evident as the years have gone by.

Some may ask, how do I explain the reason for the horrific car accident which could have left me paralyzed; let alone, potentially taken my life. My response to this is: there was a divine equation that was satisfied here as well. Unfortunately, not all of our stories will be feel good in nature. The associated actions and relative timing was such that this accident was meant to take place. I've been blessed to be able to successfully move beyond it.

Thankfully, I was open to pursuing network marketing. It provided me with a welcome and refreshing change of pace in my life. Who would have anticipated this when I was focused on earning my accounting degree in college? How about the odds for a longer-haired, somewhat non-conformist student actually completing such a degree and later on teaching one of the sections of the University's semester class offerings? It featured the same focused subject matter that was being taught during the day by three of the accounting professors that I had when I went there as an undergraduate.

Much of my background is in manufacturing accounting, performance analysis and timely and effective problem solving. It's exceedingly ironic that I've received no traditional medical direction or guidance with regard to the handling of this specific muscle disease. It's because it is so rare and so little is known about it. To this day nothing is known about its cause(s), how it can or should be treated, or if it can be solved or cured. There's another great lesson here. Regardless of our levels of expertise or skill in the handling of various matters, we may sometimes find such expertise and skills to be frustratingly inapplicable to the resolution of an issue or issues where you'd otherwise expect them to be beneficial.

We must continue to fight the good fight and never underestimate the power of prayer, while maintaining a steady attitude of gratitude. I've been experiencing an ever increasing level of bodily stiffness. By the spring of 2010, I became realistically unemployable, but had a very difficult time facing this. I find myself regularly dropping things, having difficulty bending over, struggling to pick up things near the ground and changing clothes without being close to something sturdy to lean against. In mid to late 2010, I developed vertical double vision (aka diplopia) as a complication from Graves Disease. They were considering associated, but non-exacting, strabismus surgery in the spring of 2011. My eyes were really causing me problems. I took a fall in March of 2011 as I attempted to walk into our garage and fell at the base of our stairs in June of 2011. Thankfully, the use of prescribed prisms in the lenses of my glasses have sufficiently offset the disruptive diplopia issues.

Another important lesson to be learned is that just because we may be trying to focus on dealing with one major issue, it does not mean we won't be faced with addressing some others along with it. Thanks to the professional and expeditious responses of my longtime good friend and optometrist, Dr. Randy Wild, I was able to avoid becoming blind in both eyes near the end of 2012. After experiencing some weekend symptoms, I called Randy at his home on Sunday morning, November 4th. He calmly said he needed to see me on Monday and thanks to his efforts I was able to get in to see a retinal specialist/surgeon that same afternoon.

Thereafter, next day emergency retinal re-attachment surgery was required for my left eye. Because of the level of urgency involved, the surgery needed to be conducted at a Green Bay hospital where the doctor had other surgeries already scheduled. This was 50 miles from my home and I wasn't sure how I was going to get there at that point. My wife was able to be excused from work and everything went well, my sister-in-law also offered to take me.

On the Monday before Thanksgiving, I detected a pain in the lower right side of my back. By Wednesday the pain was considerable and we were going to my in-laws for Thanksgiving. Pain had also shown up on the right side of my stomach. My father-in-law said that I could have shingles. It got progressively worse and a rash was very evident when I had Julie check my back on the Friday after Thanksgiving. Shingles were confirmed after she drove me to Immediate Care that morning. Fortunately, this did not impact either of my eyes.

Then, on December 12, 2012, I was told by the surgeon that I urgently needed to have the same surgery done on my right eye the very next day (again in Green Bay). He had told me that having this condition in both eyes was extremely rare. The previous November and December I had cataract surgeries in both eyes.

I've gotten noticeably weaker and experience considerable difficulty getting up from normal chair height, seated positions. Fortunately, I've been able to utilize a number of assistive devices to help me with some fundamental daily activities; the EZ-Step device for help with climbing stairs has been incredible, as I still have retained a manageable degree of balance.

I've found that this can be somewhat of an invisible disease to others. It's commonly overlooked and minimized because it's not well understood. Visually, I look pretty healthy if one doesn't detect the significant muscle wasting in my forearms and quadriceps or my tiny wrists. What's been very disappointing is when people I felt closer to, including some friends, do not attempt to reach out to me periodically and check in on how I'm doing. This is likely for many reasons including the busyness of their own lives. I have my weak moments and times, but usually quickly recall the tremendous willpower of my highly respected Dad fighting colon cancer, my extremely courageous brother fighting both prostate cancer and cirrhosis of the liver and my beloved and once fiercely independent Mother dealing with the daily struggles associated with dementia/Alzheimers. I've found that this snaps me out of any disruptive funk pretty fast.

There've been no medically identified recipes for success in treating this condition which comes under the umbrella of the Muscular Dystrophy Association. Most people have never heard of the word myositis. They'd associate IBM with a technology-related stock. This is what is referred to as an 'orphan disease' and it warrants increased awareness. There's no…do this or don't do that. **I tell those who'll listen that I'm not looking for sympathy, but rather am looking for understanding.** My faith in God and my wonderful wife Julie keep me strong. I'm also truly blessed to have the steady encouragement from my sister-in-law Shirley, a handful of very special friends, my cherished naturopathic health advisor Nicki and our precious little angel dog Kaylea Grace.

My own research efforts enabled me to become aware of a focused national support organization which is called The Myositis Association (TMA) in early February of 2013. It is based in Alexandria, Virginia. It features around fifty KIT (Keep In Touch) groups that are spread throughout the United States. They have area meetings typically three times per year. The associated website for this organization is www.myositis.org. Thankfully, a member of the Wisconsin KIT group which is centered in Menomonee Falls reached out to me after I had registered with TMA. I have since met nine other people living in Wisconsin (and their devoted, caregiver spouses) who have been diagnosed with Inclusion Body Myositis as well as a handful of others who suffer from one of the other two forms of myositis that are both treatable at this time. In late August of 2013, a new drug called BYM338, was given "breakthrough" therapy designation by the FDA for the potential treatment of sIBM (sporadic IBM). Technically, this is the official name given to the type of muscle disease which I've been diagnosed with. It is believed that this is now a minimum of two years away from patient availability. If approved, this has the potential for being the first treatment for sIBM patients.

Julie and I attended our first KIT meeting in April of 2013. We were impressed with the attendees' spirits and I was made aware of a personalizable business card which provides a decent explanation of the IBM muscle disease on its back. I've found that attempting to properly summarize this condition for others was always difficult. Recognizing the benefits associated with this card provided me with additional impetus to move forward with my long-time desire to write this book. I believe the stories I've told here deserve to be told because they represent honest, sincere and interesting feel good and not so feel good human interest stories. They candidly reflect memorable and divinely influenced things that have happened to me over the years. I believe that most people will enjoy reading them and be able to apply some of the lessons learned to their own lives. My hope is that they'll become more cognizant of the legitimate interwoven threads which serve a vital purpose throughout each of our lives.

My biggest turn off involves what I refer to as "could've, would've, should've" mindsets. They're basically associated with armchair quarterbacks. It's pretty easy choosing the right decision(s) when the results from the various options are already determined. I'm also frustrated by what I refer to as "if only" types. They're commonly averse to any type of risk and feature a "woe is me" mentality. This self-serving attitude provides a simplistic reason for disappointment or failure.

Many times things happen in our lives which are clearly outside of our control. You could conceivably do everything right and yet, it still may not be enough to offset the impact from something negative. There are only three ways to approach the circumstances and challenges we'll face in the course of living our lives: these are negatively, apathetically or positively. I believe that there is really only one correct choice.

Genuine belief and the refinement of a person's attitude are so critically important in everything we do. How we handle the feel good and the not so feel good incidents we each need to face will determine the types of stories we could share with others. "You have to take the bitter with the batter" was one of my Mother's many insightful and treasured messages. Her wisdom was truly infectious. God bless her.

God is always there for us and we shouldn't ever forget this fact. Therefore, DON'T EVER GIVE UP...YOU CAN'T GIVE UP.

Julie and Gary at Harrahs in Las Vegas.

Julie and Gary recognized at the Paine for 25th Anniversary.

WE WERE MEANT TO BE

Certain chance occurrences
　　Have caused our paths to meet.
Destiny has joined our hearts
　　And made our lives complete.

Not all lives that cross
　　Produce a union that is strong.
Fate can sometimes tempt
　　And then remind us we were wrong.

Fortune has confirmed
　　Our love is not a false disguise.
Love is something we in time
　　Will truly maximize.

Something rare has happened—
　　Life has given us a chance.
There is something natural
　　And true in our romance.

Days are so delicious—
　　Time is special; minds are free.
I believe our love is real
　　And we were meant to be.

　　　　　　　　—Bruce B. Wilmer

　　　　　　　　#170

How Did This Book Come About?

One early weekday morning in late July I woke up around 5:00; I didn't record the exact date but it doesn't matter. My mind became overwhelmed with what I'd describe as some very strong thoughts. The content of these thoughts was extremely distinct. They were based on an encouragement for me to definitely write the book I'd been thinking about writing for quite some time. I wouldn't even say my head was spinning because I remember being able to think and process this very clearly.

It was not long at all before the title for this book came to me as well. The definitive title had to be <u>You Must Answer This</u>. I did not get back to sleep but found myself calmly, yet enthusiastically, thinking about what had happened. This certainly both got and kept my attention. About 6:30 or so Julie came down the stairs to get ready for the day. I was now sitting up straight in the lift chair which I regularly sleep in. She had turned on a light and as she reached the bottom of the stairs she noticed I was awake and sitting up. We said good morning to each other and I then excitedly attempted to summarize what had happened. I know she was a bit taken aback when I affirmingly told her, "Julie, I need to write this book and its title will be <u>You Must Answer This</u>." She was still waking up and I don't believe she took me all that seriously.

On Sunday morning, **August 11th**, I woke up very early and just felt very driven to sit down by our computer on the main level and begin developing a detail outline for the book. The thoughts just seemed to flow through my mind and I proceeded to load them into a file I called You Must Answer This. I'd been thinking about and anticipating the content of a potential book for a long time. This enabled me to really get after it. Julie slept in for awhile and after she got downstairs by me she asked me how long I'd been up and what I was doing on the computer. I was well into the outline at this point and told her that I'd begun the formal process for writing the book. I'd never attempted to write a book before so I didn't even know what a typical formal process was. It didn't matter...I was now chomping at the bit.

It definitely wasn't planned this way, but it's interesting to note that the first time Julie and I had ever talked was on Tuesday, **August 11th, 1987**. I unconsciously began writing this book on the same date in 2013.

I'd been working diligently on the outline for some time that day and it was finally ready to be printed out for initial consumption. I gave it to the English teacher to check out. Julie sat down and closely read it over. The look on her face was priceless. She clearly had no idea of the magnitude of what I was attempting to accomplish by writing this book. I had identified the specific stories which I believed "needed to be told." She was very complimentary and it was at this point where I felt a huge "buy in" from her.

I see my rheumatologist, Dr. Eric Gowing, about once every six months. He's usually here in Oshkosh on Mondays and my next appointment with him was on Monday, **August 12th**. Since I was first diagnosed in January of 2008 with Inclusion Body Myositis there has been no medical encouragement regarding a cure; much less any effective treatment for this extremely rare and debilitating muscle disease. I told Dr. Gowing of a hopeful trial that was underway at a hospital at Ohio State University and he was quite sobering in his corresponding message to me. I told him about my intended book. He would tell you that he recognized my passion for it as I couldn't stop talking about it while I was there. He was extremely encouraging and told me I should definitely pursue completing it. He even told me the very interesting story of how he and his wife had first met. This was definitely another major Godincidence.

We'd invited my sister-in-law, Shirley, to come down for lunch on Tuesday, **August 13th**. I had recently told her about my desire to write a book but didn't get into any other specifics. When she first came into our house she turned to me and said, "I have a project for you." I told her that I had actually started the process of writing the book and asked her what she had in mind. She told me that she had a suitcase full of old photo albums in the trunk of her car. Shirley and her sister had consciously taken the considerable time to go through these albums and she wanted me to look over them and take any of the pictures I'd like to have. My original intentions were to incorporate copies of photos, ticket stubs and other types of items in my book as substantive confirmation of the associated subject matter. Here Shirley, unknowing of their current value to me, had brought six large albums; filled with numerous supportive photos which deserve to be incorporated in this book. This was just two days after I'd begun pursuing it.

Then on Tuesday, **August 20th**, I received an email from fellow IBM sufferer, James Szudzik. The FDA had just given breakthrough designation to a new drug which is believed to be potentially beneficial to people experiencing muscle wasting. Suds was so excited about this when I talked with him. I forwarded his email onto Dr. Gowing and his feedback regarding this was also encouraging. This seems to represent the brightest thing to come along yet in the effort to find help for IBM patients.

I've developed a very deep and unrelenting passion to complete this book. At the very least, it has been a tremendous catharsis for me; yet, I thought it can't end with this alone. I believe others need to read these genuinely expressed, feel good and not so feel good stories. My hope is that its readers will take the time to contemplate the interwoven nature of the people and circumstances in their respective lives. This is also intended to be a book that is laced with overriding positive emotions; whether they be associated with pride in others, appreciation of relationships, overcoming obstacles, achieving goals or being deservedly recognized by ones peers.

We've all heard the phrase, "God never gives us more than we can handle." There are times we each will question how strong we truly are. When I was given the diagnosis of incurable IBM in January of 2008, it was devastating for awhile. Thankfully, my faith in God and my wonderful wife Julie continue to give me daily strength. When something is so unknown, like this so-called "orphan disease", and is so rare that one worries that the pursuit for its cure could potentially slip through the cracks…we should still never forget that God is all powerful and is always there to give us incredible help and support. As my wonderful mother always used to say, "God works in mysterious ways." It is also right to always give Him thanks and praise.

You Must Answer This

About the Author

Gary Beyer was born on Father's Day in 1953. He hit the trifecta on that date because such recognition also fell on the first day of summer and registered as the longest day of the year. He was born in Neenah, Wisconsin; a city of about twenty some thousand people that is located in the beautiful Fox River Valley.

He received his BBA in Accounting in May of 1975 from the University of Wisconsin-Oshkosh. In May of 1980 he also earned his MBA in Accounting and Finance from there. Gary was a member of Beta Gamma Sigma National Honor Society and held directorships in the Institute of Management Accounting (IMA).

On October 1, 1988, he got married to his soul mate Julie. They recently celebrated their 25th wedding anniversary. They were united in a traditional ceremony, but it was in a non-traditional environment. Julie is in her 34th year of teaching high school English. She was also the school's drama coach for 17 years. This created a formidable duo... the atypical accountant and the atypical teacher...a match that was clearly designed in heaven. Gary and Julie do not have any children, but they've been appreciably blessed with two wonderful little dogs during their marriage.

Gary taught an evening class in Managerial Accounting at his alma mater in the Fall semester of the 1989-90 school year and proudly received outstanding feedback. He was a featured speaker in June of 1996 at the annual Direct Marketing Association (DMA) Convention in New York City and was also part of a two-person panel presentation in May of 1997 at the National Conference on Operations and Fulfillment in Orlando, Florida.

He has nearly 28 years of progressive, 'hands on' experience in manufacturing accounting; working in numerous industries during that timeframe. Gary was always well-respected as a reliable, goal driven performer who was operations oriented. He liked the diversity and the broader spectrum of contacts associated with this type of accounting work. Gary was consistently recognized for his team-building proficiency; something which he's especially proud of. At the end of

1999, he was selected as "Team Member of the Year" at his last place of employment.

Gary consciously changed his life path in the late spring of 2003. He decided to start his own home-based business. With Julie's help, he turned it into something very special for a little over seven years. He's always liked people and is highly outgoing by nature. This dramatic change was both invigorating and refreshing. They finished among the company's top 25 performers in product retailing for four consecutive years; attaining as high as ninth in 2006. Their efforts earned them three bonus cars and a rank of Coordinating Manager.

Things began to change when Gary was diagnosed with an extremely rare type of muscle disease in January of 2008. This relatively obscure condition is still considered to be both incurable and untreatable. He and Julie have been consistently told that it is progressive and degenerative. Gary's gotten steadily weaker and experiences increasing difficulty doing even simpler tasks. Here's an analyst, who's used to solving problems, that is faced with little direction and minimal encouragement. Thankfully, these determinants still must be passed through God. He's chosen to stay positive and unrelenting.

Most importantly, Gary, or Lil Gar as he's known by his friends, has always been an upbeat person who likes challenges. He's readily recognized as someone who enjoys life. He has no intention of going down easy. Gary's also a lover of music and is a long-time major league baseball fan. He's a huge Packers fan too, but his favorite team is the Milwaukee Brewers. You can ask anyone who knows him.

How About These for a Series of Incidents?

<u>Tuesday morning,</u> **September 3rd**

I had some Packers yearbooks stored in a plastic tote in the back of our basement. There was another tote which held old 45s. Julie and I try to get out and walk within our neighborhood. I brought up the point that I wanted to get down there some time and remove these things from the totes and display them. On this morning I carefully went downstairs. The effort to get at the two totes involved some careful, strategic maneuvering of other totes. I was able to get both of these things accomplished but noticed during the process of doing so that another tote had a cover that had become partially distorted and would not close properly. This tote was flush against the back concrete wall, and I figured if I'd place a couple of the other totes in a perpendicular position on top of this tote that their weight would possibly cause the cover to adequately close again.

<u>Early Thursday morning,</u> **September 5th**

Julie and I were both awakened about 4:30 in the morning by a couple of loud sounds. She was concerned that I'd fallen and called down from the bedroom "are you okay?" I said that I was and that it sounded like something had fallen either in the garage or the basement. I got myself together and first went downstairs. Sure enough, the configuration I had set up with the totes had fallen all over and blocked the aisle way. What was noticeably unusual was there was a burgundy tote that was primarily used to bring some strategic weight over the distorted cover of another tote. I'd handled this burgundy tote twice. On its side, it said frames, binders and albums and I had no intention of opening it. However, I was now forced to look into it because it was blocking the aisle way, had tipped upside down and its cover had come loose. When I removed the tote's bottom I was very surprised by what I'd find. There was an old, thin photo album, a larger photo frame which included some forgotten about pictures, and a small, flat model t-like car which held some old photos that used to be displayed on a wall in my first home. Another of the totes was interestingly lodged between the two sides of the aisle. The burgundy tote had somehow moved about five feet from where it had been located. This still makes no sense to us. Julie had come down to the basement and saw the fallen positioning of the three totes which were involved with the disruption. After I sat back in my lift chair I said, "God, I received your message." There were specific photos of people and things which directly related to some of the content already identified in my intended book. In the 'car frame' was a photo of my cousin Bob and I, in the album there was a photo of my fiancee, Bonnie, showing my friend Gary West her engagement ring at one of my outdoor birthday parties, in the large frame there was a photo of my friends Gary Ludwig, Paul Steger and myself in St. Thomas in 1985 and in the album there were two pictures of my parents flat top home prior to the later addition of a second floor. In complete honesty…I definitely would not have otherwise opened this tote. I do not know where I would have found other visual support for the four items I've referenced immediately above. You'll read about each of their importance later in the process of reading the narratives in this book.

Friday evening, **September 6th**

Julie and I went over to eat at the Chalice Restaurant. It was not that busy. Because of my muscle condition I prefer to sit at tables that feature counter top or higher stools. A couple came in and sat to the right of me at the bar. I wasn't trying to intrude on their conversation, but heard them say they lived right by the local airport on South Knapp Street. For about three weeks Julie and I were trying to remember the name of a neat two-story bar which existed about 25 years ago in that area. It featured large windows and looked out onto the airport grounds. It was really cool at night as the runway lights were always visible and when planes would either arrive or take off it provided an appealing scene. When this couple went to sit down in the regular dining room area I tapped her and we introduced ourselves. I'd heard her say "landings" and I said to Julie, wasn't the bar's name something like that? I asked the lady if she remembered such a bar and she said she did not, but she also said that she'd ask her husband and then stop back by us. When she came back she said they had lived there many years, but neither of them could remember it. The location had been turned into a Super 8 hotel many years earlier.

<u>Early Monday afternoon,</u> **September 9th**
   I'd been writing one of the narratives and headed over to the Perkins nearby to grab some lunch. There were only a few people there. I prefer sitting at a table rather than a booth and was taken to the middle dining room area. There was a gentlemen sitting by himself at a table immediately to my right. He was facing the opposite way as I was. There was a lady sitting in a booth to my left. There was another lady in a booth by the window and that was it. Both the guy at the table and myself recognized each other. He had worked in the warehouse when I worked at Miles Kimball Company. I would later see him from time to time sitting at the counter of another restaurant in town. I found him to always be an interesting person and we usually would talk for awhile. On this day, we made small talk about the weather and when he was in the service in the Philippines. All of a sudden he says, "do you remember Daniel's Edge of Town?" That was the name of the bar that Julie and I were trying to recall. I attempted to raise both of my arms and turned directly towards him. I said Jim you may not believe this, but…and explained that we'd been trying to recall this specific place's name for over three weeks. There are probably 50 to 75 or more bars in and around Oshkosh. For him to bring up the name of this specific bar that had been leveled about 25 years earlier was incredible. When I told Julie she was amazed.

<u>Lunchtime Tuesday,</u> **September 10th**
   Shirley and I arranged to go to lunch near her home in Neenah. I'd already told her about the totes incident, but hadn't told her about Daniel's Edge of Town. She was very encouraging regarding my pursuit of the book. I'd given her a copy of the outline to read and she said that I should be very proud of what I was doing. The restaurant was a favorite of ours. It was Bao Ju's. After finishing our meal we received the bill and a couple of fortune cookies. I passed one over to her and opened mine. Here's what it said, "Nothing can keep you from finishing your goals. Do it!" I was speechless and simply handed it over to her to read. She just smiled and said, "oh my God." You sure are meant to write this book. Later, when I showed this to Julie, she too was speechless for a bit. When we got back to Shirley's home we visited there for awhile. She apologized about not being able to find an

article that had been written in one of the newspapers, many years earlier, regarding my parent's home. There were also a couple of pictures with this that had been taken by a local photo studio. She had told me previously that she could picture the large envelope that they were kept in and that it had to be around somewhere. I confidently told her not to worry and that this would show up when she least expected it. She was to have a doctor's appointment the next morning at 9:30. I told her I would stop back and take her there. I was to be meeting a friend for lunch in nearby Appleton at 11:30 anyway.

<u>Wednesday morning, **September 11th**</u>

I came in the house and Shirley greeted me. She said, "guess what I found?"…and I said, the envelope with the article and pictures. She then reached over and handed it to me. What caused her to find them was she had offered her tv to both myself and her sister and brother-in-law. He'd asked her if she had any paperwork on it as to when she bought it, etc. She was looking for this when she found this envelope. Ironically, nothing was found regarding the tv. I was to meet my friend John at a restaurant that is named GingeRootz. I was telling him of the recent incidents and he was intrigued as well. Needles to say , we each were given a fortune cookie. Mine said, "Good things will come to you in due time." You must realize at this point, I was pretty in tune with everything that was going on.

It's been very clear to me for some time now that my pursuit of the writing of this book is much bigger than just my efforts alone. I've been more than convinced that I not only was meant to do it, but needed to do it. There are no fabrications here and the expression of the respective narratives comes from my heart. This is an effort of both love and gratitude. My cousin Lamont, who lives in Oklahoma, told me on the telephone that I should not only pursue the writing of this book, but that I should be sure to let God help me along the way. God is not only helping me…He's inspiring me.

Disclaimer

Each of the shared stories presented in this book are true and unembellished. They are reflections from the author's past and reveal his interpretations of various experiences, situations and circumstances that he's encountered in his life to this point. It's believed that the various photos included enhance the associated narratives with their supportive nature. There is no intent to incriminate, martyr or patronize any of the people referred to here. Likely, none of us are infallible, but we should consciously strive to do the right things and be respectful of others at all times. All the glory be to God.